My Writing Your Book

Topics That Probably Interest **You** Too

Thirtysix.org

My Writing, Your Book

Topics That Probably Interest You Too

ISBN 9798559276380

Any questions should be sent to: pinchasw@thirtysix.org.

Published by:
Thirtysix.org
22 Yitzchak Road
Telzstone, Kiryat Yearim
Israel   9083800

dedicated to the long & healthy lives of

Shlomit bat Avraham &

Amalia Rinat bat Shmuel

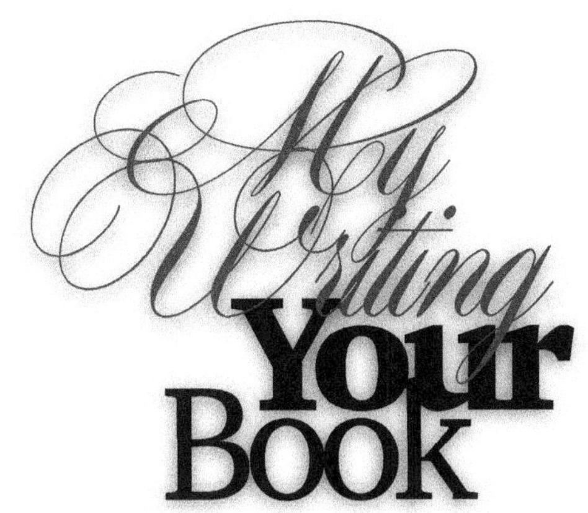

Contents

	Introduction	7
One.	Happiness	11
Two.	Money	21
Three.	Potential	33
Four	Fame	45
Five.	Food	55
Six.	Relationships	63

Seven.	Knowledge	75
Eight.	Peace	89
Nine.	Technology	101
Ten.	Entertainment	111
Eleven.	Free Will	119
Twelve.	Honesty	129
	Other Books	141

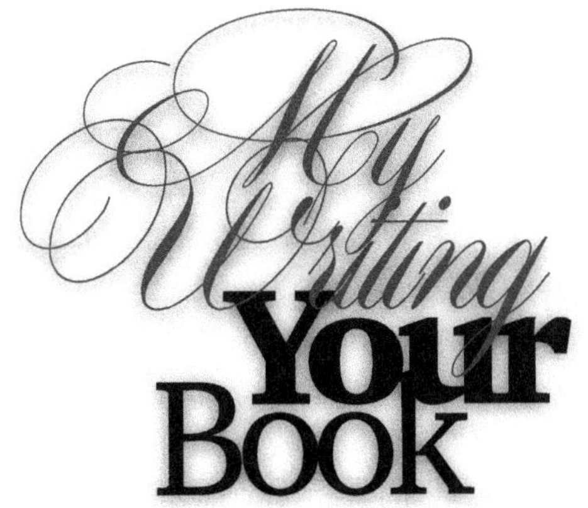

Introduction

HI! ALTHOUGH I have been aware of your presence during my entire writing career, I never openly acknowledged it. I just figured that whether you came to read my book on purpose or accidentally, you wanted to hear what I had to say. If you liked it, you'd continue reading. If you didn't, you would put down the book.

What do I have to say? Things that I want to share with people. Things that I find fascinating or life-altering. Things that I believe need to get out there, with the hope that you would be happy that I wrote the book, at least by the end of it. Was I right? I really don't know.

Most of us Torah-based authors don't know how our readers react. When I scan the shelves of Jewish book stores, I often see titles of books that make me wonder why the authors wrote about those particular subjects. Then I realize it was likely the same considerations that inspire me to choose my own topics.

It's not that we don't want tons of people to read our books. We DO. And it's not that we wouldn't like to make a good *parnassah*[1] from book sales. If ONLY! It's just that, unlike for many authors in the non-Torah world, readers and sales are not the driving forces behind writing and publishing. The Torah itself is the inspiration, with the desire to present familiar ideas or even new ones in a somewhat unique way.

But now I have a question to ask: What do YOU want to know about? What kind of books do YOU want to read? Ask not what your readers can do for you, but rather what you can do for your readers! Or something like that.

The only problem is that by the time you can answer my question, this book will already be in your hands or on your tablet, completed. The topic will already have been chosen and written in a way that I guessed might interest you.

Nevertheless, this book is different. My approach to previous books was basically to write what I wanted to say in a way that the reader could understand and relate to. My approach for this book is instead to write what I think might interest the readers in a way that will enable them to

---

[1] Livelihood.

say, "This is pretty much what I wanted or needed to know!"

Gimmicky?

Perhaps.

But I'm willing to give it a try anyhow, and hope that you, dear reader, will feel that this approach was worthwhile. Who knows? Maybe it will inspire some of you to actually send me ideas BEFORE I sit down to write the next book, God willing. Then it will truly be a book "for the people, by the people."

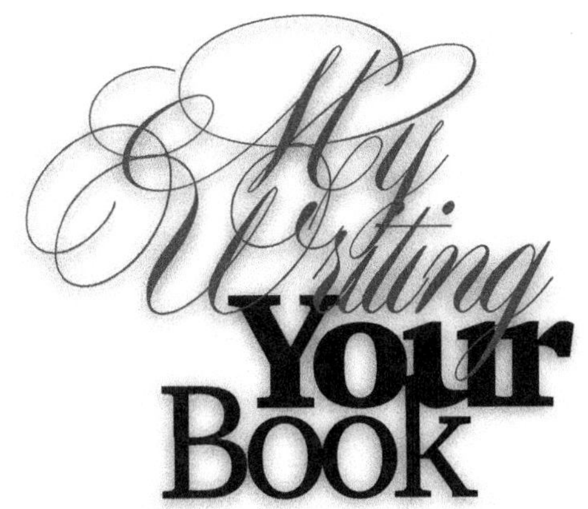

Chapter One. *Happiness*

EVERYONE WANTS TO be happy, right? Do you know anyone who doesn't? We spend our entire time on earth in pursuit of happiness in one way or another. Some people do the most bizarre things to achieve it, while others make billions of dollars promising it. Happy, happy, happy—it's all about happiness.

Oddly enough, what makes one person happy is not necessarily the same thing that makes someone else happy. Why is that? We're all human beings, aren't we? Don't we all have basically the same human needs? So how come there are so many different versions of happiness? Or are there?

Think about it for a moment. Better yet, ask someone else. Or even better, ask yourself. What makes YOU happy?

Start with obvious things, like a compliment, a present, money. Maybe it's sitting in a bathtub with the water at exactly the right temperature, lights lowered and scented candles lit, listening to your favorite music.

Perhaps it's something daring, like parachuting from 10,000 feet up, or a little less daring, like driving at 150 mph.

Is it something closer to home that makes you happy, or more accurately closer to your stomach, like a perfectly cooked juicy steak? Or something more spiritual, like getting together with family and friends, sharing good times? For many people their wedding day was the happiest, or the birth of their children.

For some people happiness may come in far darker ways. But there is no need to discuss them because they're not connected to true happiness. There is no question that such people might derive satisfaction from sadistic or masochistic behavior, but this isn't authentic happiness— we are assured of this by the very fact that EVERY human being was made in the image of God.[1] If someone derives gratification from destructive behavior, something is broken and must be fixed before he can get back on track and pursue genuine happiness.

But let's get back to you. Let's say that money is what makes you happy. What is so exciting about money? It's not the artwork and certainly not the paper it's printed on.

---

[1] *Bereishis* 1:26.

Rather it's the purchasing power of money that makes it so desirable, turning it into a doorway to other things that provide PLEASURE. Money itself is not the actual aim, but rather the things that money enables us to buy.

When someone gives us a compliment, we feel good. Why? Because it is a form of validation, confirmation that we DID good, which implies that we ARE good. Why is it important to know that? Because we WANT to be good and it's a PLEASURE to hear that we have been. Apparently it's part of our godly makeup.

But here's something surprising. We even—actually especially—delight in giving things up. We like to be self-sacrificing, provided that we agree to the reason for it. Though we may sometimes have a hard time being self-sacrificing, once we achieve it we feel rewarded. We seem to get satisfaction from that too.

We could go on and on, but the result will be the same. Things make us happy because they give us joy, and we are made for joy. We're not seekers of happiness as much as we are seekers of pleasure. Happiness just happens to be the way we measure the success of our quest.

That being so, the conversation needs to shift somewhat to the topic of pleasure itself. Clearly there are different sources of pleasure as well as different levels. It's crucial to understand this because why settle for less enjoyment when we can have the ultimate one? People who truly love being happy search for the greatest pleasure they can have at any given moment.

I'd like to think that I do.

How about you?

Whether or not you have an answer to that question, let's take a look at the whole idea of pleasure to see if understanding it better will have something to tell us about finding the greatest one of all.

Let's begin with a technical definition of pleasure:

Pleasure is a broad class of mental states that humans and other conscious animals experience as positive, enjoyable, or worth seeking. It includes more specific mental states such as happiness, entertainment, enjoyment, ecstasy, and euphoria…the pleasure principle is a positive feedback mechanism that motivates the organism to recreate the situation it has just found pleasurable, and to avoid past situations that caused pain. The experience of pleasure is subjective and different individuals experience different kinds and amounts of pleasure in the same situation. Many pleasurable experiences are associated with satisfying basic biological drives, such as eating, exercise, hygiene, sleep, etc. (Wikipedia: Pleasure)

Nothing really new here. What is interesting is not so much what it says, but what it doesn't say—what the greatest pleasure of all is. That's not actually surprising because it seems as if its most obvious source is also one of the biggest secrets of mankind, withheld FROM mankind.

Hence the variety of paths to happiness and the most chaotic history one could ever hope to avoid. People just don't get it. The pursuit of different forms of enjoyment often leads to conflict and disappointment.

Ironically the TRUE source of happiness and contentment is so personal that no one can ever take it away from us, and we can't take it away from anyone else. If everyone knew about it, people would be happier, and never at the cost of anyone else. Doesn't that sound GREAT?

So what is it?

Simple. It's YOU! The hard part is figuring out who YOU actually are. But one thing is for sure: if you happen to actually find YOURSELF, it will be so pleasurable that you will not require many of the other joys you thought you needed in order to be happy.

Does that sound obvious? Apparently not, because over the course of thousands of years not too many people have experienced such pleasure. They made the crazy and limiting assumption that who they thought they were was actually who they were. Like it or not, can you ever be someone other than who you are?

Sure, everyone acts out of character from time to time. But the way we act usually reflects who we are, right? If this isn't true for you, it would be worth getting some serious help.

Many people who get that help learn a truth about life that others fail to learn. Self-discovery is the greatest adventure of all. You're not BORN you. You BECOME you over time.

Isn't it interesting that you can't be truly happy until you ARE you? The proof that you are not yet you is that you can't seem to feel happy or at least better unless you do all kinds of fun things to inject your life with pleasure. You are dependent on external things.

A HUGE portion of the population is like that. Fun sells BIG. The entertainment industry rakes in billions of dollars supplying the average person with fun. Enjoying good food and wearing fashionable clothing are pinnacles of desire for many people. The clothing industry cannot keep up with society's lust to look good. And ALL of it is for the sole purpose of making people feel better .

"Sorry, Charlie," the old commercial used to go. "Starkist doesn't want tuna with good taste. Starkist wants tuna that tastes good." When it comes right down to it, however many substitutes for TRUE happiness there are, that is all they will ever be—substitutes. They can never last and they certainly will never do the desired job.

When a *ba'al teshuvah*[2] was asked about the difference in the quality of his life after he became religious in contrast with when he was secular, he responded. "I had a lot of fun then, a lot of enjoyment. But now I can finally say that I am genuinely happy!"

---

[2] Literally master of return; describes a Jew from a secular background who becomes religiously observant.

"But weren't you happy before, having all that fun and pleasure?"

"I thought I was at the time. But you don't know what you're missing until you find out that there is something better. That happened to me only after stumbling onto Torah!"

"But how can fulfilling commandments make you happier?" the incredulous interviewer pressed.

The *ba'al teshuvah* smiled and said, "On the outside, learning Torah and performing commandments seems counterintuitive to personal pleasure, something we do for someone else rather than for ourselves. At least that's the way it looked to me in the beginning. But the more I delved into *mitzvos*–commandments and the more I committed myself to them, the more I seemed to learn about myself. And the more I learned about myself, the more whole I felt, and more in control of the direction of my life. The happiness just seemed to flow from that, and once you learn the secret, you keep moving in that direction."

Our life can be compared to the construction of a house. When the work begins, you don't expect the house to be completed immediately. You know that something like this is a work in progress. It will take months at least until the house is finished according to the blueprint from which it originated.

Birth can be compared to the excavation of the ground. Childhood is the early construction. Adolescence adds the first floor. But it is the rest of life that completes the structure and supplies the finishing touches. We will not actually be ready to move in until the day we die.

But that's okay. This world is only the corridor to the banquet hall[3] anyway, which is the next world. The next world is where we actually live in the fullest sense of the word. In this world we prepare for the next one by building ourself to be complete, our ultimate self. It isn't until *Olam Haba*, the World-to-Come, that we'll fully receive the pleasure in being who we were created to be.

In the meantime, however, we can derive much happiness from our self-development in this world. But we need to be able to tell if we're on track—even someone who learns Torah day and night. It's easy to get sidetracked when doing anything, which causes us to lose sight of the ultimate goal. Torah has the power to perfect us, but only if we allow it to.

Therefore we get great pleasure from being who we are in essence, the GREATEST pleasure actually. It's that wonderful sense of balance we feel when all the pieces line up and work in perfect synchrony. The world can be in chaos, but internally there is nothing but peace.

We all seem to believe it exists, and religions devoted to achieving it were formed. Meditation helps a lot to find the pieces and to work on aligning them. We can do this even when we're not sitting in one place and blocking out

---

[3] *Pirkei Avos* 4:16.

the rest of the world. This kind of alignment is possible in almost every situation in life, in a world in which so many forces try to pull us in every other direction.

The first step is internalizing that as well as you may think you know yourself already, you really don't know yourself all that well. How can you? You discover this only by consciously and consistently working on it, as you would with anything new. It's something you can only learn over time, because each new day has the potential to bring out different aspects of yourself that you never knew existed.

The idea is quite abstract unless you follow a program that pushes your previously accepted limits. For example, war makes demands on people that weren't necessary during peacetime, but these demands can reveal hidden parts of our make-up. Marriage too is an ongoing program, though people don't necessarily realize that until their marriage has fallen apart.

So God gave us Torah. After all, He made us, so who better to design the program that allows us to find our true self? The Torah we learn and the *mitzvos* we do accomplish many things at the same time, but on the personal level they help us discover more about ourself, more about our moving parts.

By coming to terms with all this and by going as far as we personally can in Torah, we become increasingly aware of who we are. Then we are empowered to align our body and soul, achieving that fantastically exciting but often elusive inner peace and the incredible ongoing happiness it provides.

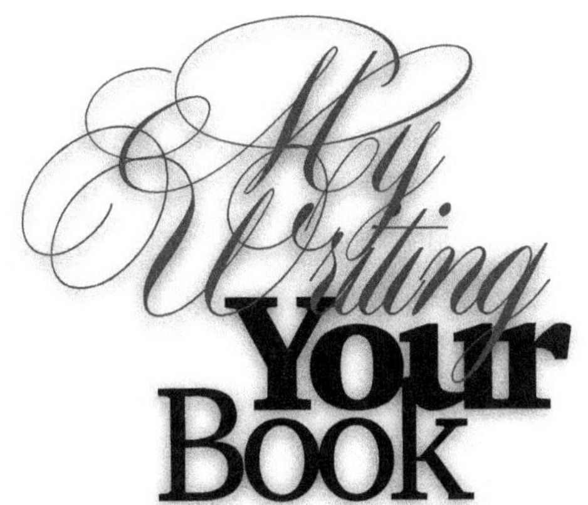

Chapter Two. *Money*

WHILE WE'RE ON the topic of happiness, let's talk about money, one of the few things that everyone seems to agree is a key to happiness.

It's clear that necessity is the mother of invention, and also the underlying basis of getting rich. If people didn't NEED things that they can't get on their own—either because they're not sure how or lack the will to do it—someone else who can fill that need has something to sell them.

We were created dependent, and that in itself generates needs. We may not always like it, especially when we have difficulty fulfilling them, but without needs we probably wouldn't care about the rest of the world or seek relationships with others. Filling a desire is one of the strongest forces driving us, and each one we satisfy makes us feel more alive.

It is important, however, to distinguish between a real necessity and an artificial one. Most REAL requirements can be satisfied with very little effort. It's the ARTIFICIAL longings, usually exaggerations of real necessities, that turn people into money-mongers, unnecessarily forcing them to devote much energy and life force into attaining their desires.

For example, if everything goes right in your upbringing, allowing you to become an adult with self-confidence, you will want to accomplish meaningful things. That's good, part of your having been made in the image of God.[1]

If something doesn't go right, however, and you grow up insecure, you may try all kinds of things to gain attention and approval. This will create a superfluous need to validate your existence by impressing others—and that often leads to the pursuit of money.

The Rambam in the first chapter of *Hilchos Dayos* says that a person should not work more each day than what is necessary to cover his basic requirements. Then for the rest of the day he will be free to pursue more meaningful goals, such as learning Torah and performing *mitzvos*, the currency of the World-to-Come.

That's what the *Chofetz Chaim* did. He had a little

---

[1] *Bereishis* 1:26.

grocery store that was open each day just until his *parnassah* would cover that one day and that day only. Then he went to learn Torah, deliberately giving business to his competitors, many of whom came to buy at his store solely to support him.

Today that would be unheard of. Close your store in the middle of the day? You'll lose so much business! Even if you earned an amount adequate for today, how can you be sure you will be able to do it again tomorrow? You have to make extra today just in case—you know, save for a rainy day!

The naysayers will also tell you that the business world today is much more sophisticated and interdependent. There are suppliers who do not share such a lofty work ethic and higher goal. They want to make as much money as they can and as fast as possible. You yourself may not care about profits but they do, and won't accept your inability to pay what you owe them—they will stop your deliveries. Then where will you be?

Some people take that into consideration and do the next best thing to closing early. They hire workers to take their place while they go off to learn. In a way it's similar to closing down, since they end up sharing profits with others, but the store is open and customers aren't disappointed.

The Talmud says that someone who has bread in his basket today and worries about what he will eat tomorrow is small in faith.[2] Does God supply people with their needs only on certain days of the week? What happened to trusting in God for your DAILY requirements? If you depend on others to fill your orders, why not God?

Admittedly that's tough. A human supplier can at least answer back. It would make us nervous to call a supplier and only get heavy breathing on the other end. It's important for us to hear someone's voice guarantee that he will not only deliver our order but do it on time.

We must also remember, however, that suppliers have reputations to worry about. They're not in business for our sake but rather for theirs. They are fully aware that if we find them unreliable, we will tell others—which is really bad for business. Thus we can be confident that they will want to enhance their reputation and increase their business, ensuring that our orders will be correct and on time.

Knowing that we reciprocate by paying what we owe, our suppliers will be even more convinced to uphold their part of the agreement. They know that if they make a mistake or deliver late, it can adversely affect our business and weaken our ability to pay them on time. Our needs keep them in business. Their needs keep them reliable.

When it comes to God, however, it's entirely different. Our desires do NOT keep Him in business. He was doing just fine before we opened shop, and He will continue to do just fine after we close down. He doesn't seem to

---

[2] *Sotah* 48b.

worry about His reputation either, so we don't have that to fall back on. To put it bluntly, God has all of us over a barrel.

Furthermore His currency is hard to find and even harder to spend. When it comes to human suppliers, a check or credit card will do. When it comes to God, money is as useless as a stone on the ground, unless it's being used in a way He likes, such as for giving charity or buying things for *Shabbos*.

No, unmarked bills don't cut it for God. He demands payment in a completely different currency, a spiritual one, one that is a lot more difficult to come up with than mere dollars and cents. His payment has to be in loyalty to Torah and *mitzvos*, with *mesiras nefesh*–self-sacrifice for both. He's not a happy supplier until He has been paid with our trust in Him.

Sounds like extortion, doesn't it? I won't give you what you need unless you trust me for it. But wait a second. Aren't there billions of people out there getting more or less what they want without having to trust in God? Don't WE get plenty of things without actually trusting in God?

Listen, people don't get EVERYTHING they think is essential, even if they're willing to pay top dollar for it. But people certainly get A LOT of it, seemingly without paying God ANYTHING. Is it any wonder that they have come to expect to receive what they want without having to trust in God in return?

This thinking is entirely wrong. It's not only a mistake

but it misses the point. The following analogy helps explain why.

Imagine a young man who graduated from college, found a job, and is earning a good salary. But he refuses to move out of the family home because he prefers to freeload there and have more money to buy things he enjoys. With marriage not too far off, he wants to spend his money for pleasure while he can.

His father is irked by this. Not by the freeloading per se, but because he feels that his son should be saving money for his future. It's important to have fun but not at the cost of a happy, less stressful future. Knowing his son well, he is aware that telling him that will only result in arguments.

Therefore the father takes a different tack. He tells his son that since he is making good money, he will have to pay rent. "Of course I won't ask as much as a regular landlord would," the father says, "but it would be nice if you contributed to our financial burden now that you can."

At first the son thinks his father is joking. "Charge a family member rent?" he thinks to himself. "No one does THAT."

But when he realizes that his father means business, his response turns to outrage instead. "How can your charge your son rent in his own home?" he shouts, threatening to move out. And though his father feels bad and realizes it will cost him some closeness, for the good of his son he does not capitulate.

The son for his part checks around and does the arithmetic, quickly realizing that as absurd and embarrassing as it is to pay rent to one's own father, the alternative is worse and far more expensive. Who would cook for him and do his laundry if he were living on his own? Begrudgingly he pays the rent and continues living at home, even getting used to it after a while.

Some time later the son becomes engaged and the wedding follows shortly after. The *simchah*[3] is beautiful and there are certainly no hard feelings between father and son, especially since the father is footing a good portion of the bill.

Just before the *chupah*,[4] the father takes his son aside and hands him an envelope. The son looks at his father in surprise and opens it. It contains quite a large check, and the son is both ecstatic and confused. Why so much, and why now?

He looks at his father, who has a knowing smile on his face. It's the tipoff that makes the son all of a sud-

---

[3] Rejoicing, joy; joyous celebration.
[4] Canopy beneath which a marriage ceremony is performed; often used to refer to the marriage ceremony itself.

den realize that the amount is exactly the total of the rent he had paid. The inquisitive look on his face draws an explanation from his father.

"Did you think all that time I was actually charging you rent to stay in your own home?"

"I did. What else could it be?"

"I was worried you'd spend too much of your money and regret it later, once you got married and started your own family. I made that mistake when I was your age. I also knew that if I told you to save your money, you'd just be resentful."

"You're probably right," his son agreed.

"So I used the rent as a cover to save some money for you, and here it is!"

As tears welled up in the son's eyes, he said, "I owe you a HUGE apology, *Abba*,[5] and a TREMENDOUS thank you."

"For what?" his father asked.

"First of all, for doubting you and questioning your normalcy for charging your son rent…And also to thank you for saving me from myself. I am truly grateful to have this money now. Clearly I would have spent most of it on things I wouldn't even be able to remember!"

Although this is an analogy, it's an accurate one. Our

---

[5] Father.

present world is the only one we can see. We've heard about the World-to-Come, the same way the son heard different things about marriage. But being so far off in the distance and outside personal experience, it is a reality to which we have trouble relating.

Like the father in the story, our Father in heaven knows what to expect in the future. He knows its importance, and why it is so crucial that we use our time in this world to build up for the next one. If we spend all our money before we take a trip, what will we have left to enjoy after we land? As the rabbis say:

> This world is like a corridor before the World-to-Come. Rectify yourself in the corridor in order to be able to enter the banquet hall. (*Pirkei Avos* 4: 16)

Our Father in heaven also pretends to charge us rent. He too takes a portion of our earnings and puts it away for later. We have a *mitzvah* to give *tzedakah*,[6] to use part of our hard-earned salary to help the less fortunate survive. We're giving it to someone else, right? We're helping God out with our money, right?

Wrong. The money may go to the poor person, but the *mesiras nefesh*, the ONLY currency of the World-to-Come, goes right into our *Olam Haba* bank account. When we get there, God will give it back to us and say, "I

---

[6] Charitable giving; literally righteousness.

thought you could use this better now, when it is worth so much more—FOREVER!"

And *ma'aser?*[7] We tithe our produce to help God take care of the *kohanim,*[8] *levi'im,*[9] and poor. He says it really belongs to Him, but we earned it. He's just taking it for Himself, and we give it to Him for the promise of being even more successful in the future.

Wrong again.

ALL our earnings belong to Him. As the verse says, "'The silver is mine and the gold is mine,' said the Lord of hosts."[10] He's just being VERY generous by giving us most of what we earned, thanks to His help. As the Talmud says, "The entire world is sustained by God's charity,"[11] which He grants us so we can earn more reward in the World-to-Come.

This is not only true about sharing our wealth, but it applies to ANY *mitzvah* we do. *Mitzvos* take our time and expend our energy. But this time could be spent solely on temporal gain with no long-term benefit, and the energy easily wasted on superficial pleasures. God, acting as the loving Father that He is, has given us a program to make us

---

[7] Tithe.

[8] Priests.

[9] Descendants of the tribe of Levi. In Temple times they served as musicians and singers, and assisted the priests.

[10] *Chaggai* 2:8.

[11] *Brochos* 17b.

save time and energy for the life we will later live and want to live, with everything we ever earned.

We call it *yesurim*–suffering, but God calls it earning a living for a world where "your days may be long,"[12] referring to the world that is entirely long. When the verse says "that it may be well with you," it means in the world where all is well.[13]

But alas, our perspective has been corrupted over time by *Eisav*[14] and his descendants. *Eisav* pursues wealth for its own sake and because of the pleasure it can give him here. And that's okay—for *Eisav*. Only righteous gentiles go to the World-to-Come,[15] so the others have to be paid off in this world for the good they have done.

But not *Ya'akov*[16] and his descendants. Their *parnassah* may be earned in this world but it is not for this world.[17] It may appear as dollars and cents in this world, but it is measured in terms of *mesiras-nefesh* dollars in *Olam Haba*. We're unfortunately not always smart enough to know this or sufficiently sharp to remember it. But God is and does, by giving us His Torah to live by.

"Who is a wealthy person? Someone who is happy

---

[12] *Brochos* 22:7.

[13] *Chullin* 142a.

[14] Esau.

[15] *Avodah Zarah* 10b.

[16] Jacob.

[17] *Kiddushin* 39b.

with his portion."[18] Is this talking about actual material wealth? Perhaps, but not as much as it is talking about our REAL portion: Torah, *mitzvos*, and *mesiras nefesh*, THE money of the World-to-Come.

> Happy are we! How great is our portion, how pleasant is our lot, and how nice is our inheritance! (Preliminary Morning Prayer)

---

[18] *Pirkei Avos* 4:1.

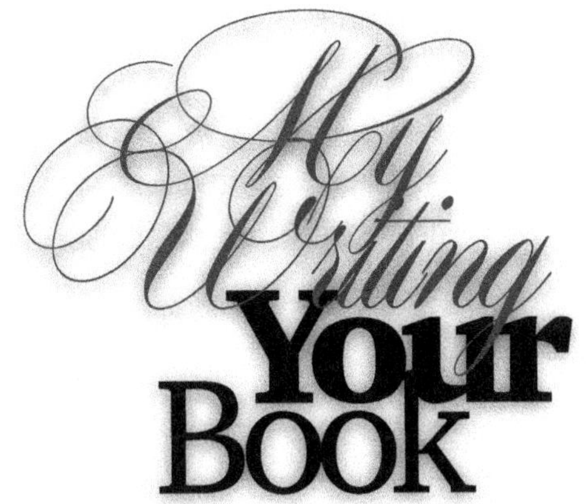

Chapter Three. *Potential*

POTENTIAL IS AMAZING. One day you can be watching your one-year-old child innocently playing with blocks on the floor, and later on that same child—now an adult—is leading a country of millions of people or perhaps performing bypass surgery to save someone's life.

The knowledge necessary to do these things had to be acquired from the outside. There's only so much we can figure out on our own in a single lifetime. Knowledge is cumulative, and each generation builds on the contributions of past ones. But the potential to use that knowledge and do more or less with it is something that we are born with.

Can you imagine what it would be like if there were a

way to know your latent abilities early on in life? I mean REALLY know your capability, ALL of it, with certainty. Just think what an average person could accomplish in a single lifetime, and what kind of world we might have. If people who had low self-esteem could see their aptitude for good, would they choose good over evil instead of the other way around?

Since it's not possible to know our potential, the only way we can get a hint of it is by pushing ourself. And even then we may only push as much as is necessary to get by, rather than to accomplish as much as we possibly could. We might be impressed by our successes, but we'd be far more impressed by what we could have achieved had we tried a little harder.

Why does it make a difference? Because we have an innate need to use our abilities. Animals only need to survive—that's what they're programmed to do. They have built-in computers that constantly monitor their vitals, and if they match up with the pre-programmed expectations, then everything registers as good and they continue to exist.

We human beings on the other hand sometimes feel physically great—we're well fed and have strong hearts and good bodily functions—but we're not happy. Everything is all right physically but we may not be doing anything meaningful. If somehow this registers in our brain, it can agitate us, making us sense a lack. We don't feel as if we're accomplishing something.

We clearly have a level of consciousness that other beings do not share. Not only are we aware, but even self-aware. And not only aware of our own self, but we see ourself within the context of a world that promotes achievement. Even if we were on a deserted island with no one to be compared to, we'd still feel the drive to accomplish, to use our talents.

One thing for certain is that this drive doesn't come from the body, but from the soul. A couch potato proves that, ignoring the impulse of the soul and sitting in front of a TV set for hours on end with beer in hand, or endlessly surfing the web just because it's there. As one very wise man said, "Wasting time is partial suicide."

We are not machines and we need some R&R. But we're not supposed to take a break just for the sake of a break. The respite is supposed to allow us to recharge our batteries in order to go back to accomplishing as soon as we can. This isn't an addiction, obsession, or enslavement. It is living.

Unless, that is, your drive to accomplish is solely to finish at the front of the pack. If personal accomplishment matters little besides propelling yourself to the front, then it's no more meaningful than doing nothing at all.

Life isn't about accomplishments.

It's not about fame.

It's not about reward.

It's about using personal ability as much as possible. Competition is fine as long as it's only against ourself. We strive, but only for our own sake. We achieve because it validates our life to us. The fact that others inspire us or compliment us is nice, but not necessary aside from confirming that we are on the right track.

> *Rebi* said: Which is the straight path that a man should choose for himself? One which is an honor to the person adopting it, and [on account of which] honor [comes] to him from others. (*Pirkei Avos* 2:1)

Courses should be established solely on the topic of aptitude—how to find it and how to develop it. In a sense that is what all courses are about, since inborn capability allows us to succeed in learning. But by not discussing the topic of potential directly, we neglect the main point of why we try to do anything, thus overlooking how much competence is available.

People choose professions and lock themselves into a single course for life. They choose favorite activities and close out opportunities to succeed at others. Although they may excel, it's in very limited ways—but they still call it success.

Once upon a time there was a term used for a clever person who was good at many different things—Renaissance man. Today people specialize, striving to be experts in their chosen fields. They may be experts in something, but they are certainly not experts at life, since they ignore a great deal of proficiency in favor of a single pursuit.

How do you assess the invisible? How can you see what might develop from what has yet to develop at all? There are a few givens that show up early, like body structure or a clever mind. But many people improve much later in life, becoming stronger by working at it or smarter because they enjoy or learn to enjoy learning. All that is hidden potential. Some stumble across it while many others completely miss it.

What would help is a capability meter attached to each one of us to see how much promise we have and how much of it we are using. We were able to successfully develop ways to measure blood pressure and heart rate. Surely GOD could have made us with a meter that measures our potential.

In the good old days that was something a prophet was capable of determining. You could bring your child to him and ask, "How should I raise this child?" Seeing the child's hidden talents, the prophet could direct the parent to teach each child according to his innate ability.

We don't have prophets anymore, and child psychologists are distant seconds. So is there anything we can do to fulfill potential—either as adults or for children who are growing up? Or are we stuck just going with the flow, like so many billions have done over the millennia?

There actually is a way to deal with the issue—by seeking greatness. If we train both ourself and our children to be great, then we will would have to draw on our gifts to accomplish it. It requires setting goals and trying to attain them. That will definitely reveal skills that we either have or don't.

A lifetime of this approach will surely bring us a lot closer to using our skills. We just have to decide to do great things relative to ourself and devote the effort it takes. It doesn't have to be relative to anyone else because we are all different and have different faculties. We just have to plan to do what is great in comparison to ourself, which is always significant to God.

It doesn't matter whether or not anyone else notices the greatness. In fact it is probably better if no one notices, to avoid its leading to ego issues and making a mess of using potential. Craving for attention? That shows need for approval and doesn't make us great. Greatness requires independence from craving for attention and all the other issues involving ego.

Okay, that solves one problem but it creates another: How do we know when we're GREAT? Does being great also include being a capable thief or a great liar? Is there an objective greatness?

Let's start by asking what being great brings to mind.

When we use that term to describe people, we usually mean that in our eyes they excel at something. It's possible that they're great in just one area—he's a great athlete or a great investor—and be lousy at just about everything else. Lots of people are good at something. To be great at it, you have to do it much better than others.

What about being a great person? Does that imply a

global greatness? No. Consider excellence in sports. This one area that may not interest many people, and someone outstanding in it isn't classified as great in general. Likewise the abundance of outstanding businessmen, all doing business differently, perhaps working just enough to get by, some of whom excel. That's not greatness, but rather doing a good job in a part of life, not in life itself:

"What do you do for a living?"

"I'm a lawyer."

"I didn't ask you about your profession. I asked what you do to live!"

"I'm not sure what you mean. Aren't they the same thing?"

"Not at all. Your profession is to help you live. Living is doing whatever you must to enhance the spiritual quality of your life. You want to be able to look back on your life and know that you did whatever you could to be the best you possible—from your Maker's point of view."

"Hmm. I never looked at it that way."

Even though we were born a particular way, we can improve on that considerably. As we meet person after person, we notice that in our eyes some are superior to others and seem to have done more with their personal givens, making us think of them as great.

This definitely is not about judging the true greatness

of other people—because we can't possibly do that. We don't know their starting points or what they have gained or suffered along the way. If anything, the Talmud says that we have to judge people to the side of merit,[1] even if at the same time we have to watch them out of the corner of our eye to protect ourself.

This is rather about appreciating that certain personality traits are more appealing and productive than others, depending on the situation. For example, being caring is a wonderful trait but not when the recipient of the care wants to hurt others. Discipline leads to productivity, but it's not appropriate when the other person needs mercy.

That's also part of human greatness—being able to accurately assess a situation and respond to it in a suitable manner. It makes you seem in touch with reality, and clever about how you navigate it.

Moral consistency in others earns our respect and admiration. And though some would argue that this is due to nurture and not nature, life seems to indicate otherwise. True, a child who grows up in the jungle will not know morality, but he won't be respected as a great person either.

We may require nurture to know what being good is, but it is our nature that allows us to appreciate the importance of being so. It is something inbred that permits a certain kind of morality to ring true for us, although we pos-

---

[1] *Shabbos* 97a.

sess the ability to reject it. That's the power of free will we were given to use for earning our portion in the World-to-Come.

That nature is the soul. The soul is a divine spark, holy by definition. The body is but the vehicle we use to get around and accomplish things in this world, but the soul is the engine that drives it. The brain may be a part of the body, but the mind is a function of the soul, and as we notice from people in comas, a mindless brain is little more than a lifeless computer.

The most hardened criminals have souls or they wouldn't be alive. Their souls are holy sparks, just like all others, no matter how unholy the actions of the lawbreakers may be. That makes it hard for them not to sometimes act like good people despite their crooked lifestyle. It's due to those holy sparks. It isn't just society that says they are wrong, but something inside does too. Hating their inconsistency, they harden themselves on the inside, and it is reflected on the outside.

This is one reason *teshuvah*[2] is closed to someone who does a sin with the idea of repenting for it afterward.[3] It isn't a punishment for cheating. Conscious sinning, especially if done to such an extent that someone plans his repentance in advance, changes a person's self-perspective.

Sinners therefore close the door to *teshuvah* on

---

[2] Usually translated as repentance; literally return.
[3] *Yoma* 85 b.

themselves. By going against their inner sense of right and creating inconsistency, the result is a hardening of their hearts, making *teshuvah* seem less important and even unnecessary. Hence the Talmud's warning.

> Rav *Huna* says: Once a person commits a transgression and repeats it, it is permitted to him. Can it enter your mind that it is permitted to him merely because he has sinned twice? Rather, say that it becomes to him as though it is permitted. (*Kiddushin* 20a)

This is what happens when people ignore their potential to be productive, which is a soul-based drive, and instead actualize their powers to be self-destructive, which is a body-driven impulse. The farther down that road people go, the more difficult it becomes to return. Thus aptitudes are constantly being squandered.

My *rosh yeshivah*[4] would frequently tell us, "You can be GREAT!" In the beginning I was convinced that he was just trying to encourage us to at least be good. As they say, if you don't shoot for the stars, then you never leave the mud. And who wants to remain in the mud?

But after hearing it over and over again, I began to believe that it was what he really believed. The idea of doing great things went from impossible to feasible to imperative. I can attest that many of his students went on to do

---

[4] Head of a *yeshivah*.

great things. Over the years it has also helped me to accomplish more than I might otherwise have achieved, given my previous acceptance of mediocrity.

So we may not have prophets or potential meters these days with which to measure ourself and our aptitudes before deciding our path in life—but that doesn't mean that we shouldn't sit down and try to intuit what kind of potential we might have in order to accomplish great things. If nothing else, it encourages God to help us find out and get us on the path to personal fulfillment.

That idea potentially has a lot of merit!

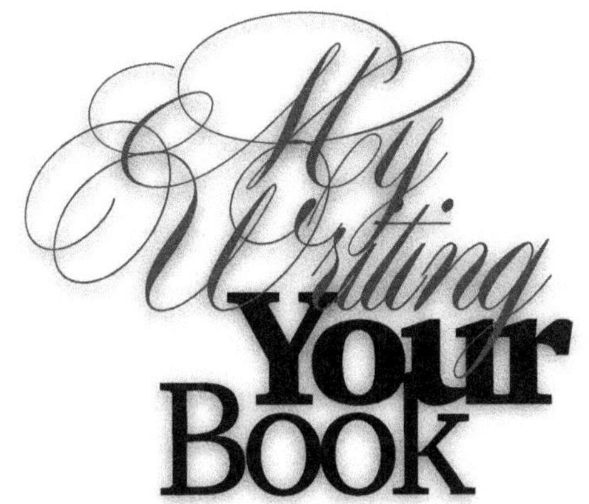

Chapter Four. *Fame*

A PROMINENT PERSON WAS QUOTED as saying, "When I started becoming more well known, I began to worry about being conceited. I had seen it happen to many others, people I thought would NOT have been affected so adversely. I liked the attention but not the conceit. So I turned to God and said, 'Please let me be successful but not famous. I don't know how that works, but you're God. You can make ANYTHING work.'

"And He did! My success increased, but not my fame…at least as far as I knew. I didn't get much feedback from anyone, and at times I wondered if I were doing everything only for myself. Then I found myself saying, 'Okay, God, maybe just a LITLE fame.'"

The rabbis teach that honor is bestowed on those who run from it. An honorable person is one who honors others, not one who seeks honor for himself. If you go after it, something is lacking in you. If you flee from it, then you are probably humble and, most important of all, emotionally independent. You don't need the approval of others to prove that you are worthwhile—you just need Torah.

We all need to feel we're valuable. We NEED to know that we count. The only time we require others to recognize it is when we ourself are unsure. Either we have yet to learn our place in history or have lost track of it. So we ascertain what others value and try to get their attention by catering to that.

People who know their intrinsic value don't require the admiration of others to validate their existence. They may appreciate the feedback of others for the sake of quality control, especially when they're doing something for someone else. But their self-worth remains self-defined. They want to be famous only to themselves.

The starting point of self-approval is a single fact that no one can change:

> And God created man in His image; in the image of God He created him… (*Bereishis* 1:27)

Consider a person who is appointed to be the king's representative. Whatever expectations he previously had of himself have to be upgraded. If he were to do something attention-grabbing in the past, people didn't care very much. But now, when he is representing the king, people not only notice his actions but they evaluate and criticize them. That's a price people pay for being important.

So before we look at ourself in the mirror and devalue our existence, we have to understand that we do not have the right to do that. We cannot give back a gift bestowed on us when we were created. We can abuse the gift —for which we will have to answer later—but we cannot return it, at least not while we're still living. God has imbued EVERY human being with HIS image, and by definition that makes each of us His representative on earth.

If we all truly took this single fact to heart, we'd never need the approval of others, but only of the King, God Himself. We would take justified pride in this lofty elevation over all other aspects of Creation and seek ways to do it honor.

Such aware people would have only one question at the beginning of each day: What can I do to live up to this great merit? And likewise one question at the end of each day: How well did I measure up as a *tzelem Elokim*, one made in the image of God? This would be the only concern, because everything else that is important would be a function of this reality.

However, if you take God out of society, then you remove your *elokus*, godly image. This has been a strong trend lately in Western society, so is it any wonder that society as a whole has become more insecure, more fame-driven? People think they have been clever by "killing off" God when in fact all they have really done is killed off their most important and self-assuring element. How smart is THAT?

People who cross over from that world into the one of *tzelem Elokim* can notice the difference early on. To the extent that they get the overall message of Torah, that is the extent to which they will find their focus shifting from trivial societal competitiveness to a process of sincere self-evaluation, based on the standard of *tzelem Elokim*. If they compare themselves to others, it would be only to learn how to do a better job of being a *tzelem Elokim*, since everyone has something to teach about it.

Fame and fortune. These two words sum up the dreams of billions of people throughout history. The people who built the Tower of Babel wanted to make a name for themselves. This can be understood on many levels, including that of Kabbalah, but at the end of the day it really means the same thing: to become famous, to be adored by others.

The concept of adoration isn't foreign to Torah. But it is never applied to a person—or at least it shouldn't be. The admiration is supposed to be of accomplishment and of representation. A *gadol hador*[1] or a *rosh yeshivah* has the esteem of his followers because of all the Torah he knows

---

[1] Rabbi who is great in his generation and serves as an authority in Torah law.

and the extent to which he lives by and for it.

Because these followers cherish Torah, they have come to know that there is much to learn and the value of knowing it. They realize how much self-sacrifice it takes to learn so much Torah—and even more the devotion to live by that knowledge. When they see people who do this, they appreciate to what a great extent they have become representatives of God. THIS is what inspires the respect of their adherents.

Not having to impress others or even want to is truly wonderful. That doesn't mean that you don't have to care what others think about you or what you do. You certainly do! There are *mitzvos* that govern our relationships with other people and define our social responsibility.

But none of these *mitzvos bein adam l'chavero*—between someone and his fellow—say that you achieve self-validation through the opinions of others. That's strictly between you and God, and really between you and yourself. You have to know what is right, how well you can live up to it, and the effort you makc to do so. Period.

Because let's face it, people admire many things in others that they don't deserve credit for. To begin with, as the Talmud states, *mazel*[2] plays a major role in a person's life. Yes, we can mitigate our fortune, but we can't ever completely change it. And just to mitigate it takes a lot of spiritual work that many are not prepared to do. So their

____

[2] Destiny.

mazel remains as it is.

What many might call a self-made man may not be that at all. For every person who succeeds at what he does, there are many others who tried the same thing—perhaps working harder—but do not succeed. It just isn't in their *mazel* to make it as the apparently self-made person did.

It's not just *mazel* that plays a role in material success. History does too. Our individual life occurs within a framework of world history that has its own needs, based on the long-term goals of Creation. The master plan always takes precedence, which means that some people who should succeed don't, while others who seem unworthy to succeed actually do.

What about physical appearance? Genes determine a lot about our physical stature, and who gets to choose or develop those? Yet people are willing to idolize some people who just happen to get enough right ones to make them attractive, while ignoring others who don't.

It's curious that God created the world this way. Why should it be that some people never have a problem with weight although they eat whatever they want, while others can't indulge even a little without tipping the scales? Why are some people too tall, some too short, and some just right? Why do some people get to keep all their hair until they die while others lose it long before? No wonder so much jealousy and competition exist!

It's true that you need darkness in order to appreciate light, but is it fair for short and unattractive people to be sacrificed so that we can appreciate the opposite? Even if many of the less attractive types tend to be some of the finer people in society SPECIFICALLY because they are not particularly attractive or popular, they may not feel it's worth it.

The opposite type raises questions as well. If being born with physical assets is for the purpose of challenging people to be spiritual despite their advantages, then that too seems unfair. Such people may be prone to adoration and miss the whole point of life, being distracted from it for reasons beyond their control.

If the naturally attractive subsequently pamper themselves, it is still a function of a lifestyle thrust on them, one which may hinder their entry into the World-to-Come. Sure, they're getting a lot of attention now. But it's the NEXT world where people will truly want attention—for the right reasons—and that's where it truly counts. It won't be for what people are inclined to get it down here. The desire then will be for what God wants to give them solely because He wants to give it.

If you think about it, REALLY think about it, both circumstances—physical assets or lacks—are actually for the same purpose. The person who feels left out because he doesn't have what society appreciates and the one who receives recognition from the world are both fighting similar battles. Underneath their physical skin and features is basically the same set of bones, and we're all here to accomplish the exact same thing—which is surely not to become arrogant.

We even have a special blessing in the *Shemoneh Es-rei*[3] against arrogance and the arrogant, the ones who think they know better than everyone else by virtue of their own success and talents.

It doesn't mean that they can't be more qualified than others for certain jobs and responsibilities. God made them that way specifically with talents for those jobs and responsibilities. But as the rabbis cautioned in *Pirkei Avos*, the wise man is the one who learns from all people, smart or not. If anything, his own personal greatness is humbling, because he doesn't see any reason for God having blessed him more than others.

People have to believe in God to be humble. How can they avoid arrogance if they are convinced that they made it to the top of the pyramid by themselves? With that certainty, even those who don't mean to become arrogant can't really help it. That's why the Torah has all kinds of *mitzvos* built in—like fear of God—to help us with that, but we ourself still have to fight against arrogance.

Arrogance is definitely not a function of the soul, but rather of the body. The soul is a piece of God and is therefore God-aware by virtue of its self-awareness. Doubt, if it exists, is in the mind—but it's a function of the body, not

---

[3] Literally 18, the original number of blessings in the central prayer in Judaism, although a 19th blessing was later added. Also called the Amidah–Standing because it is recited standing.

the soul.

Just ask a convert—not to Judaism but rather from agnosticism to God-belief. Find out what changed for him and why. How is it possible that one day he had a difficult time accepting the notion of God and then another day it was easier?

Certainly maturity is a factor. As we get older we usually mature intellectually as well as physically, and can better appreciate the importance of some ideas over others. Additional information can make a HUGE difference because extra evidence helps the brain to more easily assess the reality of situations that come up.

But many people still do not change their opinions. On the contrary, they move farther away from God, not closer. What is the additional factor that makes newfound believers different from others?

Humility. Something happens to humble them. It doesn't have to be humiliation per se—it might have to do with their predispositions. A number of factors can lead up to it, but somehow particular information gets past the body's defenses and registers in the brain. "This makes sense—it's worth further investigation."

Once THAT happens, idea after idea comes until such a person sees or hears enough to say, "This is too logical not to be true. I can either plead cognitive dissonance and turn my back on what is probably the truth, or I can face the music and make the necessary changes."

And they usually do.

Something remarkable and extremely purposeful happens to such people: their bodies become less dominant and their soul more prominent. They become less fixated on the material aspects of everyday life and more spiritually inclined. Their goals also change, and they find themselves acting more *b'tzelem Elokim* than ever before.

Then these awakened people wonder how they could ever have been any other way.

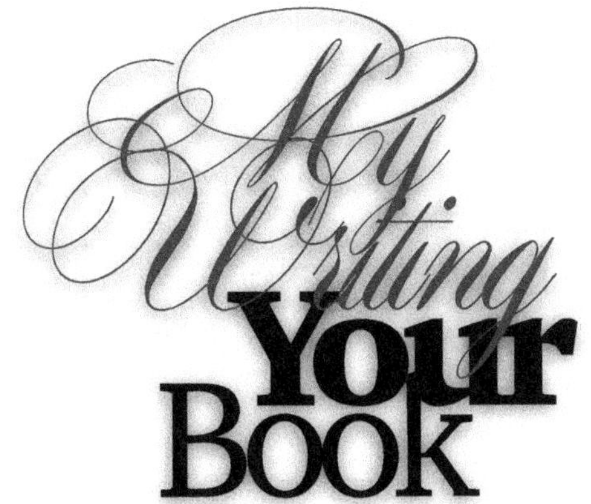

Chapter Five. *Food*

I LOVE FOOD. Who doesn't? In my entire life I think I have only met ONE person who didn't enjoy food. Everyone else either LOVED eating and did it regularly or hated being overweight more than he LOVED eating and therefore dieted frequently. Only that one person literally ate solely because he had to, and I feel both sorry for him and envious.

Sorry for obvious reasons. Envious because that non-eater has one up on the rest of us. In his opus magnum *Yad Chazakah* the *Rambam*[1] sets out the rules about life according to Torah, and one of them is eating only enough

---

[1] *Yad Chazakah, Hilchos Dayos*, Ch. 3.

to stay healthy. While many have difficulty doing this, especially in today's society of plenty and the spectacular, this non-eater has to push himself just to eat enough to be healthy.

Remember that we, meaning the Jewish people, are here in this world to do one thing and one thing only: earn reward for the World-to-Come. Yes, there is much to do and enjoy in this world, and it can be extremely distracting. But if it doesn't somehow fit into the program of increasing or at least maintaining a Jew's future portion in the World-to-Come, then it is meaningless.

Or worse. Someone could find himself eating away at his eternal portion now. In this world pleasure is limited and finite. In *Olam Haba* it is the opposite. That is why the rabbis have STRONGLY advised us to stay on track and not get hung up in the corridor.

All PHYSICAL pleasure we derive while navigating this corridor should be incidental. Even the pleasure of eating must never be a goal of its own, unless it is a means of enhancing a *mitzvah*, such as making *Shabbos* more enjoyable or increasing the joy of a newly married *chasan*[2] and *kallah*[3].

And if not? Although the rabbis have advised against it, is it really wrong? This, taken from the confessional on

---

[2] Bridegroom.

[3] Bride.

Yom Kippur,[4] seems to say so:

> And for the sin which we have committed before You by eating and drinking.

Perhaps this is only talking about abusive eating or eating food with a questionable *hechsher*?[5] No! According to what has been said and especially considering the following discussion, it seems to refer to ANY unnecessary eating.

Rav *Tzaddok Hakohen*[6] in his landmark work *"Pri Tzaddik"* provides a very important insight into eating and consumption in general, in connection with a somewhat unique *halachah*.[7] The Talmud says that anyone who eats on *Erev Yom Kippur*,[8] the ninth of *Tishrei*, is considered to have fasted for two days in a row, both that day and the next, *Yom Kippur*.

Why? Because eating on the ninth makes the state-

---

[4] Day of Atonement.

[5] Kosher certification.

[6] Rav *Tzaddok Hakohen* Rabinowitz of Lublin, Poland (1823-1900), was a significant Jewish thinker and chassidic leader. One of his famous works on the weekly Torah reading and holidays was called *Pri Tzaddik,* so he is often referred to by this title.

[7] Laws and ordinances whose principles are the 613 commandments in the Torah given by God, but whose applications are decided in every generation when necessary.

[8] Evening of *Yom Kippur*.

ment that "I enjoy eating, but I will be fasting tomorrow on *Yom Kippur* because God has commanded me to, not because I want to." This joins the eating to the fasting and has the same effect as fasting for two consecutive days. The *Pri Tzaddik* explains that kabbalistically it actually counts as 26 fast days altogether! It doesn't get much more bizarre than that.

Why the unusual calculation? Rav *Tzaddok*'s answer takes us all the way back to the Garden of Eden and the very first sin, which involved, of all things, illicit eating. God said:

> ...But from the Tree of Knowledge of good and evil you must not eat, for on the day that you eat from it you will surely die. (*Bereishis* 2:17)

Instead of obeying the command, however,

> ...she took of its fruit, and she ate, and she gave also to her husband with her, and he ate. (*Bereishis* 3:6)

It was an *achilah sh'lo b'kedushah*, an unholy eating, according to *Rav Tzaddok*. When Adam and *Chava*[9] ate from *Aitz Hada'as Tov v'Ra*, the Tree of Knowledge of Good and Evil, it was not to satisfy any positive divine purpose but rather their own, as it says:

---

[9] Eve.

And the woman saw that the tree was good for food and that it was a delight to the eyes, and the tree was desirable to make one wise... (*Ibid.*)

But eating on *EREV Yom Kippur*, says the *Pri Tzaddik*, is an *achilah sh'b'kedushah*—a holy eating—since it is done purely for the sake of a *mitzvah*. By eating on the ninth of *Tishrei* to emphasize our willingness to fast as commanded on the tenth, we rectify the sin of the very first man and woman, as we should be doing whenever we consume ANYTHING in this world. And this is PRECISELY what the *Rambam* instructs:

Whoever walks in such a path all his days will be serving God constantly; even in the midst of his business dealings...for his intent in all matters is to fulfill his needs so that his body will be whole to serve God. Even when he sleeps, if he retires with the intention that his mind and body rest, lest he become ill and be unable to serve God because he is sick, then his sleep is service for the sake of God, blessed be He. On this matter our sages have directed and said: "And all your deeds should be for the sake of heaven." This is what *Shlomo*[10] declared in his wisdom: "Know Him in all your ways and He will straighten your paths" (*Mishlei* 3:6). (*Yad, Hilchos*

____

[10] Solomon.

Dayos, Ch. 3:3)

That's one level of the discussion. There is a deeper one as well, and it has to do with *nitzotzei kedushah*, holy sparks.

You might have thought that the smallest thing in Creation is the quark because it seems, for the time being, indivisible. But as small and invisible as a quark is to us, there is something more fundamental to existence and it isn't even physical! It is a holy spark.

What's a holy spark?

A holy spark is an individually packaged amount of God's infinite light. These sparks exist in everything, animate and inanimate, and are the life force of everything that lives. But even though we need them in order for us to exist, they do not belong down here on earth and must be released and elevated to their appropriate place in the spiritual realm.

But how do you elevate something you can't see or know is real? By making use of them. It can be the most obvious form of consumption like eating, or a less obvious type, such as using energy to perform some activity. Just sitting in one spot utilizes sparks too, though in a more limited manner. Their elevation depends on the extent or lack of holiness of the activity performed.

Kabbalah details the entire process of elevating the sparks, and it is complicated. But it is also essential, and the rectification of Creation depends on ALL the sparks which God put into the world being elevated to where they belong, as per God's plan for Creation and man.

So when we eat anything, we are consuming the holy sparks that allow it to exist. The more sparks food has, the healthier it will be for us. As the food is digested, the sparks are liberated from their physical carrier and spread throughout our body, giving us energy to perform activities or simply to live. Then the sparks are expended and freed to rise spiritually to where they belong. Creation is now that much more rectified.

Provided, that is, the sparks are used in a holy manner. Frivolous activities do not elevate sparks very much, and certainly don't contribute to world rectification. When too much of THAT happens, God usually steps in with some kind of cataclysmic event to put Creation and the elevation of sparks back on track.

Just one more question to ask for now. What happens to all the sparks that we elevate by consuming in a holy way in this world? Something truly amazing. They actually become part of our portion in the World-to-Come. The amount of our ETERNAL pleasure depends on the sparks we elevated.

This is something to remember as we play the role of consumers in this world. Anyone can eat. But it is the person who eats for the right reasons and in the right way who rectifies the sin of sins, and reaps the benefits of doing so in this world and especially in the next one.

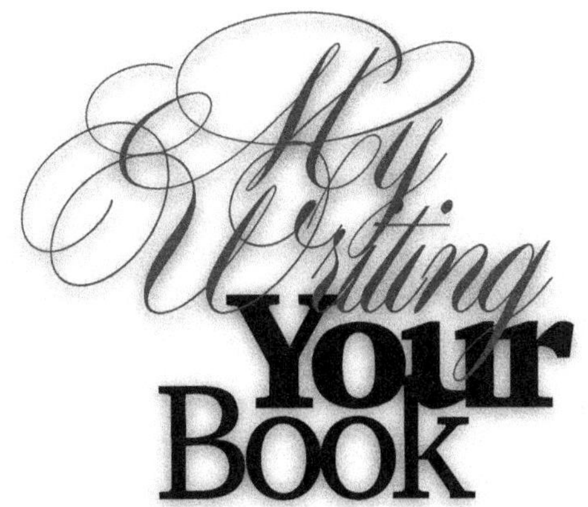

Chapter Six. *Relationships*

YOU CAN'T LIVE with them, and you can't live without them. At least that's the way it often seems with relationships. A fundamental part of life, they sometimes come at a very high cost, especially emotionally. There is really no way of knowing up front just how high the cost of a relationship will be, and the element of risk is always present.

Why do we even need relationships? The first man was created alone, and he seemed okay with that until he noticed that the other creatures, who were so different from himself, came in pairs.[1] This made him think that

---

[1] *Rashi, Bereishis* 2:21.

perhaps he too should have a partner. That's when God put Adam to sleep and performed surgery to create another one like him in female form.[2] This also made it clear to the angels—who had previously mistaken Adam for God—that he was merely flesh and blood.[3]

Chava's creation changed everything. Had she not been created, *Adam Harishon*[4] would probably not have eaten from *Aitz Hada'as Tov v'Ra*—the Tree of Knowledge of Good and Evil. It was she who was compelled to eat the forbidden fruit, later giving some to her husband to eat as well.

On the other hand, the first man would have lived a very lonely existence without her. Unless God made someone else for him, he would have been alone forever. And had God made another man, they probably would have killed each other fighting for control of the garden.

Perhaps the biggest change was the need to create and maintain a relationship, not just with someone else, but with someone else who was different. *Chava* was different in form, different in thinking, different in terms of needs. The animals lived in their own world and *Chava* was meant to share Adam's.

To help the first husband get off to a good start, the first wife came with instructions.

---

[2] *Bereishis* 2:21.

[3] *Rashi, Bereishis* 2:18.

[4] The first man.

And man named all the cattle and the fowl of the heavens and all the beasts of the field, but for man, he did not find a helpmate, *aizer*, opposite him—*k'negdo*. (*Bereishis* 2:20)

That might not sound helpful until the Talmud explains it.

Aizer k'negdo: If he merits it, *aizer*; if he does not merit it, *k'negdo*. (*Yevamos* 63a)

According to the Talmud, the role a wife plays depends on the role her husband engages in first. HE'S the determining factor in the relationship. SHE'S flexible, which means that a woman can be her husband's partner in success if he brings that out in her, or she can be his stumbling block if his treatment of their relationship leads to that.

We see this from the very beginning. When *Chava* disobeyed her husband's directive to not even touch the tree, which led to the eating and breaking of God's command, was she helping Adam or working against him? Given God's response to what they did, we'd have to say the latter.

The Talmud's explanation, however, raises a question: Where had Adam failed his wife so as not to merit her help? The Torah tells us:

And the woman said to the snake, "Of the fruit of the trees of the garden we may eat. But of the fruit of the tree that is in the midst of the garden, God said, 'You shall not eat of it and you shall not touch it, lest you die.'" (*Bereishis* 3:2-3)

And you shall not touch it: She added to the command; therefore she came to diminish it. That is what is stated: "Do not add to His words" (*Mishlei* 30:6). (*Rashi*)

And the snake said to the woman, "You will surely not die. (*Bereishis* 3:4)

You will surely not die: He pushed her until she touched it. He said to her, "Just as there is no death in touching, so is there no death in eating." (*Rashi*)

She ate. And here we are, 5780 years later, still living everywhere BUT in Paradise as a result. But if it really were *Chava* who expanded the command by adding the part about touching, then how could the snake have tricked her into eating it? She would simply have said, "No, you silly snake. I said we can't touch it. God said only that we can't eat it. Therefore touching it does not cause death, but eating it surely will. Get lost before you make me do something I shouldn't do!"

It is obvious that for the snake's ruse to work, *Chava*

had to believe that God had commanded them not to touch the tree. If we search the Torah, however, we don't find any place where God did that. So where did the idea come from, the one that opened the door for the original snake to cause almost six millennia of exile for mankind?

From Adam. It was Adam, her husband, who added a fence to the Torah. He was worried that his wife would be more likely to eat the fruit if she touched it, since the distance from the hand to the mouth isn't very far. Appreciating the seriousness of the sin and realizing how easy it would be to err, he told his wife not to even touch the tree.

The only problem was that he failed to explain to *Chava* one tiny detail that could have altered the course of human history, making the writing of this essay and so many others COMPLETELY unnecessary. He neglected to mention that the fence was his and his alone. In failing this crucial responsibility, he transformed his wife from an *aizer* to a *k'negdo*.[5]

It is amazing that so much destruction could result from such a SEEMINGLY insignificant detail. It certainly emphasizes the responsibility a teacher has to students to make sure they accurately receive what was given.

In fact the Talmud tells the following story that makes a similar point:

---

[5] *Drushei Olam Hatohu, Drush Aitz Hada'as, Siman* 3.

Rebi Perida had a certain student whom he would [have to] teach 400 times, and [only then would he] learn [the material]. One day they needed [*Rebi Perida*] for a *mitzvah* [after the lesson. *Rebi Perida*] taught [his student 400 times as usual], but [this time the student] did not learn [the material. *Rebi Perida*] asked him: "What is different now [that you are unable to grasp the lesson]?"

He answered: "From the time that they said to the master that there is a *mitzvah* [for which he is needed], my mind was distracted [from the lesson] and every moment I said, 'Now the master will leave, now the master will leave.'"

[*Rebi Perida*] told him: "Pay attention [this time] and I will teach you, [and know that I will not leave until you have fully mastered the lesson]."

He taught him again an additional 400 times. (*Eruvin* 54b)

Lest someone think that this was no big deal, the Talmud concludes:

A divine voice went out and said to him: "Is it preferable that 400 years be added [to your life] or that you and [the rest of] your generation merit the World-to-Come?"

He said: "[I prefer] that my generation and I merit the World-to-Come."

The Holy One, Blessed be He, said to the angels: "Then give him both…" (*Eiruvin* 54b)

Just as it is remarkable that Adam's not telling *Chava* the source of his "rabbinical decree" caused expulsion from the Garden, it is significant that *Rebi Perida*'s extra 400 efforts to teach his student gave him an extra 400 years and also brought an entire generation to the World-to-Come. It makes the strong point that when you help others, you really help yourself at the same time.

In fact there is something about helping others stand on their own two feet that God really likes. That is why there is *chesed* and there is *gemilus chassadim*. The word *gemilus* comes from *gamal*–camel, a symbol of independence because it is the only animal that can travel for days in the desert without water.

This is why the Hebrew word for weaning, *vayigamel*, has the same root. Weaning starts the process of making a baby more independent of its mother, or an addict from anything he has been dependent on.

Chesed is about doing a nice thing for someone else. *Gemilus chassadim* is about helping others to achieve more independence, to become more themselves. And according to the *mishnah*, it is one of the three pillars on which the world stands:

Shimon Hatzaddik was one of the last of the men of the Great Assembly. He used to say, "The world stands on three things: the Torah, the Temple service, and *gemilus chassadim*." (*Pirkei Avos* 1:2)

Clearly this idea does not apply only to a relationship between husband and wife. It defines the dynamic of EVERY kind of relationship, male-female, male-male, female-female, parent-child, sibling-sibling, even human-animal. EVERY relationship is supposed to be give and take, and will run smoothly only if the giving builds up the other side.

Dependent people build dependent relationships. An emotionally dependent person will be more focused on taking than giving. A pleasure-driven individual will be looking toward others to provide pleasure. These types can be so focused on what they are not receiving from the relationship that they overlook what they are not giving. This leads to the failure of the relationship.

Sometimes the failure is total, resulting in divorce of some kind. Sometimes it is partial and a couple stays together but remains emotionally divorced. After all, where WAS Adam when the snake found an opportunity to talk to his wife, setting in motion catastrophic events? Many marriages do not make it to divorce court, but they're sometimes not far from it.

Even worse is when people remain in a relationship solely in order to take. That is when they become manipulative, trying to eliminate whatever independence the other side might have had. Little is more destructive for

BOTH parties.

The Torah tells us that we were made in the image of God. Countless commentaries over the ages have tackled the question of what that actually means since God, not being corporeal in any way, doesn't have an image to begin with. One thing for certain is that "image" refers to a capacity that other created beings do not have.

Another such capacity is our ability to care for others even more than we care for ourselves—not just family but even strangers. Animals are programmed to care for their young and are willing to sacrifice for them. That's not a choice they make but rather a response to their built-in computer.

Humans, however, can prefer not to give but give anyhow. They can feel a pull to think about themselves first and still put others before them—and feel good about it. We share a survival instinct with the animal world, but our world also includes spiritual survival, and it is THAT unique capacity that enables us to resemble our Creator.

One reason God created a wife for *Adam Harishon* was that, as mentioned above, the angels confused him with God.[6] God does not have another like Him, so when Adam was joined by a counterpart, it became clear that Adam was human, not God. Seemingly it was a downgrade.

Not really. On the contrary, until the creation of *Cha-*

---

[6] *Rashi, Bereishis* 2:18.

va the potential for relationship was merely that—a potential. Adam may have looked like a god to the angels, but he certainly didn't act like one. To do that, he had to be able to care about someone outside himself, and to help someone else become the most he or she could be. From this perspective, *Chava* was an upgrade.

The irony of it all is the one thing that so many people have known but not quite grasped. Everyone knows that when you give to others for THEIR good, you receive for your OWN good. Not because you plan it that way—because it doesn't happen if you do.

It works because God, in His infinite wisdom and mercy, likes to reward the supporters of His plan for Creation both in this world and the next one. Therefore He made available what we ourselves most need spiritually through our giving OTHERS what they most need spiritually.

Every soul knows that. It's the body that gets in the way. Though self-centered people may obtain what they WANT, they never get what they NEED. What's the pleasure in having the former if they lack the latter?

This is why, like *Eisav* before them,[7] they spend so much time trying to find things that will make them happy. In the meantime, the selfless person enjoys personal completion and contentment from a fraction of a fraction of what *Eisav*-like people acquire. It may look like just the

---

[7] *Rashi, Bereishis* 33:9.

opposite on the outside because contentment or turbulence on the inside doesn't always show.

You can't beat the system, no matter how smart or how talented you are. Arrogance is certainly not going to help. God made the world and God made man. Man was created alone to make the point that our main relationship is between us and God, and no one else. But He followed up with another human to make the point that we need other relationships as well.

We are here to also relate to other people. That can mean something as simple as a friendly hello when passing them. But it principally means doing for them what God has done for us. He has given us life and a fair bit of independence to go along with it. He has provided us with the opportunity to make something of ourselves in this world and the next one. And when we help others do the same, God is never happier about the actions of His most important handiwork.

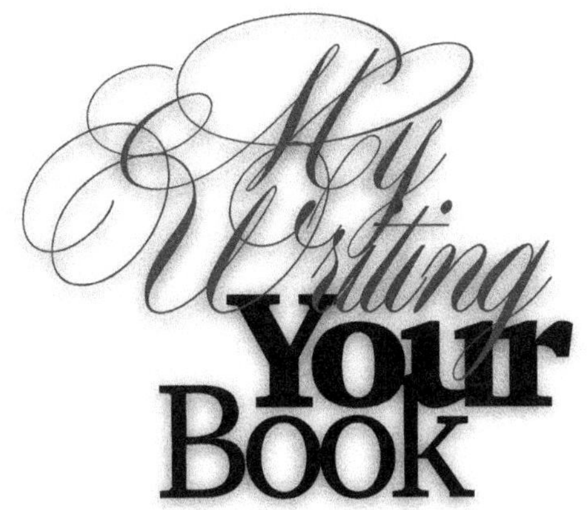

Chapter Seven. Knowledge

A LITTLE BIT of knowledge is a dangerous thing. At least that is what some people say. But it is certainly not literally true because knowledge in any amount is wondrous and wonderful. The more you have, the better off you tend to be. It only becomes dangerous when it is abused, and that has more to do with the quality of the person than the quantity of what he knows.

The *yeshivah* I went to was big on outreach. Our *rosh yeshivah, Rav Noach* Weinberg, *zt"l*, started a *teshuvah* movement, and was intent on training outreach professionals as quickly as possible. Since many of the young men he ended up working with were themselves *ba'alei teshuvah*, it took more time than he felt he had. So he developed a program to get the students started sooner.

His plan created controversy. How could someone who barely knew the *aleph-bais*[1] begin teaching others who knew even less? Wouldn't that lead to misinformation or turn potential students away from Judaism because of a misrepresentation of God's Torah? Wouldn't it unnecessarily expose the under-developed would-be teachers to situations beyond their capabilities?

For these reasons Rav *Noach* emphasized the need to "know what you know," and not to go beyond it. He taught us that it was okay to be honest and say that we didn't know when asked questions for which we had yet to learn the answers. He said that was a lot better than acting as if we knew more than we really did.

It was great advice, though not always easy to follow in the heat of a discussion. But more often than not we did stick to the rule, which allowed many a work-in-progress *chozer b'teshuvah*[2] to share what he knew and positively influence others along their paths to become dedicated outreach professionals.

Rav *Noach* did not just emphasize the know-what-you-know ideology when it came to sharing knowledge with others. He also told us to make sure to apply it to ourselves as well, which meant that for our own sake we

----

[1] Alphabet.

[2] Literally "returning in *teshuvah*," to indicate that someone is still on the path to full repentance.

should never assume we understood something better than we really did. "Clarity or death!" he was wont to say, and "five-finger clarity!"[3] This defined our approach to learning and knowledge.

As I grew in Torah knowledge, I was amazed at how true the *rosh yeshivah*'s words were. There were many people with half-baked or completely wrong opinions about Torah Judaism—as I once had—because of incomplete or incorrect information. And even more amazing was that they were certain they had it right or at least right enough until I showed them how they had missed the point.

Many people who otherwise knew a great deal tended to clump together ideas that did not belong together. Each of separate points can have its own merit, something that is lost when they are dealt with as a single, often misguided idea.

"No, this means this," I would explain, "and that means that," and they would later wonder why they hadn't figured it out on their own. But once they saw it, they attained a clarity that often changed their opinion for the better about God, Torah, and those who live by it. "I think, therefore I am" may be true. But thinking itself must be an art if it is going to accomplish more than just confirm one's existence.

---

[3] When you are as clear about an idea as you are of the five fingers you can see on your own hand.

There are levels of excellence in virtually every activity. Anyone can paint, but only a few can paint masterpieces. Anyone can write, but not everyone can write best-sellers. You can get started with a basic understanding of something, but it takes more than that to excel. Although talent makes it easier for some, only discipline and practice make it possible for others.

It is no different with respect to knowledge, which we seem to take for granted. Everyone is always learning something on some level, and if you learn enough, you might be called a genius or expert in your area of expertise.

But the art of thinking isn't so much about gaining the adulation of others as it is about a kind of mental alchemy. For knowledge is only knowledge, and potentially very dangerous unless it is transformed into something far more godly, something we call wisdom. And that clearly doesn't happen by itself.

Even in Paradise there were two separate trees, *Aitz Hada'as Tov v'Ra*—the Tree of Knowledge of Good and Evil—and *Aitz Hachaim*, the Tree of Life. Though everything originates from the same source much higher up in the spiritual world, things become distinct from one another down here. *Ya'akov* and *Eisav* came from the same spiritual root, but they were literally like day and night, good and evil.

After Adam disobeyed God's command not to eat from *Aitz Hada'as*, he was certainly not any wiser, except for the realization that he had made a catastrophic mistake.

That resulted in his losing access to *Aitz Hachaim* and the awesome wisdom it provides its consumers.

You might think that there is not much difference between knowledge and wisdom, but history shows otherwise. Looking back over the past almost 6,000 years, we can safely say that periods of history have been anything but safe, despite the great accumulation of knowledge. Wisdom has NOT been the guiding light of mankind's decision-making.

There are many ways to discuss the fundamental difference between *Aitz Hada'as* and *Aitz Hachaim*, knowledge and wisdom, some quite kabbalistic. For now let's just say that knowledge is the accumulation of facts and information, while wisdom is the synthesis of knowledge and experience into insights that deepen one's understanding, thus improving the quality of life. And though it seemed as if *Aitz Hada'as* would provide both knowledge and wisdom, in the end it provided only the former.

People may dream of living forever, but many are definitely better off not living that long. That's certainly what God concluded when He greatly shortened our life span. Long ago people lived healthily for 1,000-plus years. Today few reach 100 years, and even fewer with a robust sense of life.

"What is the point," God likely thought, "of letting people live so long if they are simply going to add to their already long list of sins and wasted life?" Thus for example the Torah says that God took *Chanoch*[4] before his time for this very reason.[5]

There is even a Torah law, called *ben sorrer u'moreh.* It commands the *bais din*[6] to execute a specific type of rebellious child before he has actually done anything deserving of capital punishment. "Take him from this world," God says, "while he is still young and merit-worthy."[7]

So as desirable as a long life might seem to us, it is only desirable to God if the time is WISELY spent. In fact from God's perspective it is better that a person live a short and meaningful life than a long and meaningless one. Best of all, of course, is living a long AND meaningful life—and that is where wisdom comes in.

For the most part knowledge has been used to help us better understand the PHYSICAL world of which we are a part. We use it to our PHYSICAL advantage. Society has thus become more knowledgeable as a whole, but not at all wiser. Hence Einstein's remark, "Two things are infinite: the universe and human stupidity; and I'm not sure about the universe."

He wasn't talking about the world's level of knowledge, which was increasing exponentially in his time. He was talking about different perspectives on life, which dic-

---

[4] Enoch.

[5] *Rashi, Bereishis* 5:24.

[6] Rabbinical court; literally house of judgment.

[7] *Devarim* 21:18.

tate our response to everything, even Einstein's work. He didn't expect everyone to be a genius, but he was disappointed by how stupid so many people seemed to be.

Wisdom is the cure for stupidity. It is that special outlook on life that allows you to use knowledge to its utmost advantage. And what is remarkable is that you don't have to be a genius to have wisdom. In fact some of our wisest people have also been some of the least knowledgeable as far as technical, secular knowledge goes. How is that possible? They knew how to extract the inner truth from what they did know.

In a conceptual sense, wisdom is the silver lining inside the knowledge cloud. General knowledge deals with the HOW of existence. Wisdom deals with the WHY, and not so much the TECHNICAL reason but rather the PHILOSOPHICAL one. It's the "why" that gives people the reason for their having been created and what they are supposed to do while living in this world, according to their Creator.

The physics professor finished writing a complex equation on the board, and felt he had sufficiently explained it and all its parts. However, when he turned to face the students, he noticed one raised hand, which he acknowledged.

"But why?" was all the student asked.

The professor, assuming that the student needed further clarification of the mathematics, patiently reviewed the equation he had just taken such great pains to explain as clearly as he could. When he finished, he turned to the student to be sure that he had succeeded in answering the question this time. He was dismayed to see the same confused look.

The student proceeded to describe his difficulty. "I understand the equation on the board. I'm asking you WHY it is like that."

This time the professor, finally understanding what the student meant, replied rather sharply. "This is Physics 301," the goal of which is to learn and understand the TECHNICAL implications of such equations. The answer to your question can be found in the philosophy department."

When most scientists and mathematicians ask about anything in Creation, they mean it technically. They want to understand why the universe, past or present, dictates the world to be the way we see it and how it operates as it does. Rarely are they in search of the ideological messages that Creation might have to teach about how to live life to its fullest from the Creator's viewpoint.

As the *midrash* says, when God decided to make Creation, He used the Torah as His blueprint.[8] This means that every aspect of Creation—physical and spiritual—is an expression of Torah philosophy, God's perspective on life

---

[8] *Bereishis Rabbah* 1:1.

for us. If you sufficiently reverse-engineer anything in Creation, you should be able to arrive at the Torah concept that gave rise to it.

Avraham Avinu did exactly that, which is how he found God long before God ever spoke to him. According to the Talmud, *Avraham*—purely by understanding the nature of the world—was able to construct the *mitzvos* we were to be commanded hundreds of years later at Mt. Sinai.[9]

This put *Avraham* on the same philosophical page as God. It also earned him the right to become the father of the Jewish people, while the rest of the world was fulfilling Einstein's statement about the stupidity of mankind. *Avraham* may have liked science too but he was more fascinated by the "why" that gave rise to it, because THAT knowledge improved the QUALITY of his life.

Moshe Rabbeinu[10] too. The Torah records his response to the burning bush as if it were simply something that anyone whose curiosity was piqued might respond to as he did:

> So *Moshe* said, "Let me turn now and see this great spectacle, why the thorn bush does not burn up." (*Shemos* 2:3)

---

9 *Yoma* 28b.
10 Moses, our Teacher.

What did he plan to do? His lab was miles away, and he hadn't brought his camera with him. Even had they been accessible, did he plan to take a sample for scientific analysis if the bush didn't stop burning?

That not what he meant. *Moshe* was actually asking, "If everything is from God and a function of divine providence, what is the reason for God putting this spectacle in my path? What am I supposed to learn about life from it? Let me approach it and see if I can discern the message behind what I am witnessing."

His answer was forthcoming when God spoke to him from the bush and appointed him *Moshiach*[11] in his generation. His reaction to the burning bush was a test to reveal his spiritual makeup and approach to life. These were to become the basis of his role in history, which was to lead the children of God out of Egypt and to Mt. Sinai to receive Torah—the greatest and best explained repository of divine wisdom known to man.

Clearly the Written Torah is not the end of the story, but rather the beginning of it. As *Ben Bag Bag* has revealed:

> Turn it over, and [again] turn it over, for everything is in it. (*Pirkei Avos* 5:22)

EVERYTHING is in the Torah, the blueprint for Cre-

---

[11] Messiah.

ation. But he also added:

> Look into it; and become gray and old in it; do not
> move away from it, for you have no better portion
> than it. (*Pirkei Avos* 5:22)

Ben Bag Bag is telling us that Torah is the only real
way for a Jew to go in life. But he is also telling us that the
wisdom about life it has to offer will not simply jump out at
the person who seeks it. Like a precious diamond, it has to
be intellectually AND spiritually mined.

We understand what intellectually mined means. To
access Torah wisdom, you have to "turn it over and [again]
turn it over." This means examining it and all its attendant
resources in order to go as deep into a Torah idea as hu-
manly possible. God wouldn't have given us Torah on four
levels if He had intended otherwise.[12]

But what does it mean to spiritually mine something?

> God saw that the light was good, and God separated
> between the light and the darkness. (*Bereishis* 1:4)

> He saw that the wicked were unworthy of using it,
> and therefore set it apart for the righteous in the fu-

---

[12] The symbol for the four levels [of Torah] interpretation is the Hebrew word *Pardes*, the letters of which stand for *Pshat*, *Remez*,
Drush, and *Sod* (*Sha'ar Hagilgulim*, Introduction 11).

ture time. (*Rashi*)

He made a separation in the illumination of the light, so that it would not flow or give off light except for the righteous, whose actions draw it down and make it shine. However, the actions of the evil block it, leaving them in darkness, and this itself was the hiding of the light. (*Sefer Haklallim, Klal* 18, *Anaf* 8, Os 4)

And there you have it, why the silver lining of knowledge is such a rare commodity that Einstein felt compelled to express his disappointment in mankind's level of intelligence. If you want to become more knowledgeable, you need only go online and read. Whether good or evil, the same knowledge is accessible to anyone with a computer or a book.

But not wisdom. That is the light within the light, the soul within the soul, which can only be accessed with a SPIRITUAL key. As it says:

The beginning of wisdom is the fear of God. (*Mishlei* 9:10)

There's no other way, no shortcuts, no cheating. You can't fake it, and the best way to know if you try to do that is to consider how little your knowledge mystically transforms into wisdom, like silver into gold. A person is either in or out, committed to a Torah approach to knowledge or not.

If and when God is satisfied that the former is the case, that the person is indeed a truth-seeker to the end, then He will open His treasure house of infinite wisdom to him. And once inside, it becomes impossible to go back because as the first man and woman learned the hard way, that is DEATH itself.

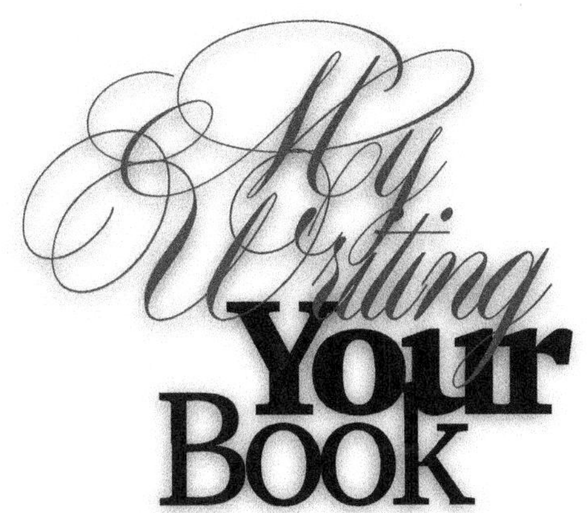

Chapter Eight. *Peace*

THERE ARE MANY things that provide great pleasure in life, and peace has to be at the top of the list. Even though we haven't really been exposed to it in recent memory, people dream of WORLD peace. So far there seems to be one war or another going on somewhere in the world at any given time. But that hasn't stopped people from trying to experience their dream.

Perhaps they will get an A for effort, but they're probably not going to achieve much more than that. It seems that world peace will remain elusive for now, especially since most individuals can't truly reach the level of personal serenity. How can people in personal turmoil resolve world turmoil? How can they do it even if they believe they have inner peace?

What is INNER peace anyway? In simplistic terms, it means that nothing bothers us deeply. None of the unsettling negative emotions are in play, leaving us with a feeling of bliss. In other words, at least most of the time we don't have an upsetting care in the world.

But what happens if we find out that something is wrong that we didn't know about?

"Why didn't you tell me?" the irate businessman asked his secretary. "I could have done something to limit the damage!"

She explained. "The truth is that I came into your office to do exactly that, but you were leaning back with your eyes closed and hands behind your head, feet on the desk, and you looked so peaceful I didn't have the heart to ruin it."

Does the businessman then say, "Oh, in that case, thank you very much for being so thoughtful"? Or does he say, "I'd rather have known about the problem so I could respond to it, instead of enjoying some brief mental quiet."

True, we might feel some temporary calmness if we're unaware of a looming crisis. But something about being human seems to make us need to justify unearned benefits we receive. If we can't do that, it doesn't feel right…almost as if we stole something not ours. That can even lead us to feel GUILTY that we had the pleasure in the first place. Although getting away with a crime can be a relief because it may spare us from punishment, in no way does that excuse the crime. We can even end up feeling uneasy about it.

That helps explain why some people who have yet to become hardened by corrupt behavior sometimes turn themselves in, after they apparently have escaped being caught. Not only can they not enjoy what they stole, they can't enjoy their legitimate achievements either. It's as if an inner voice keeps saying, "A crook is a crook, even when you're not being one."

The word *shalom*–peace hints at this. In the Hebrew spelling the core of the word is *Lamed-Vav*, and according to Kabbalah THAT always alludes to one of the holiest parts of Creation, *ohr haganuz*, the hidden light of Creation, which preceded everything in Creation and is the basis of it.

This is one of the best known verses in the Torah:

And God said, "Let there be light!" and there was light. (*Bereishis* 1:3)

What is not as well known—or known at all—is the nature of this light. The Torah itself tells us that the sun, moon, and stars were not put into place until Day Four. *Adam Harishon* did not discover fire until *motzei Shabbos*.[1] Thomas Edison would not make the first lightbulb for another 5,640 years. So what light is the Torah referring to?

---

[1] Evening after the Sabbath.

Whatever light it was, it evidently didn't stick around for very long:

> God saw that the light was good, and God separated between the light and the darkness. (*Bereishis* 1:4)

> He saw that the wicked were unworthy of using it, and therefore set it apart for the righteous in the future time. (*Rashi*)

And that's how the primordial light of Creation became the hidden light of Creation. Other lights can also be abused by the bad guys, but God seemed less concerned about them than about this particular light. So He hid it...in a manner of speaking.

Kabbalah explains that the hiding was partial—only from evil people. Just as physical light requires a physical capacity to see it, spiritual light requires a spiritual capacity to see IT.

Just as physically blind people cannot see physical light, spiritually blind people cannot see spiritual light:

> He made a separation in the illumination of the light, that it should not flow or give off light except for the righteous, whose actions draw it down and make it shine. However, the actions of the evil block it, leaving them in darkness, and this itself was the hiding of the light. (*Sefer Haklallim, Klal* 18, *Anaf* 8, *Os* 4)

If your ability to enjoy true *shalom* depends on your accessing the *ohr haganuz*, and your ability to access the *ohr haganuz* depends on your level of spiritual sensitivity, then tranquility is a function of spiritual sensitivity. Spiritually desensitized people cannot know inner peace in any real or lasting way.

What does that mean? There are a lot of spiritually desensitized people out there who seem to have a pretty good handle on it. If they don't, then what do they have instead?

An example will help clarify it.

Let's say someone is having a difficult day and needs to vent. So he phones his best friend who happens to be having a wonderful, calm day. After two minutes of conversation it becomes clear to the friend why he was called, and it begins to ruin HIS day. Resentful, he politely and quickly hangs up as soon as possible, leaving the caller feeling more dejected than before.

Without true inner peace we can't always handle negative emotions—our own or those of others. Sometimes we don't even have the time or the emotional strength to offer a shoulder to cry on. We may feel bad saying no, regardless of whether or not the person doing the complaining is a habitual dumper. A friend in need is a friend...

Some people make conscious decisions to maintain their own personal serenity, if necessary at a cost to others. They build for themselves balloons of life—capsules in this new age of corona—and intend to soar above anything that can remotely threaten their tranquility.

There is another phrase for this approach: cognitive dissonance. This means that people shut out anything they don't want to confront, though they know they should deal with it. It's an attitude of "what I don't know can't hurt me." But it can and often does hurt them. When enough people suffer from cognitive dissonance, down the line it can lead to catastrophic disasters, including world war.

A classic case in point is British Prime Minister Neville Chamberlin's inability to grasp the plans of Hitler, *ysv"z*,[2] to conquer all Europe, including England. After meeting with the fascist leader, Chamberlin returned home and giddily stated that there would be peace, despite all the incredible signs to the contrary.

There was once a joke about such peace in the Middle-East. How do you make a lion lie down with the lamb, the quintessential symbol of utopian peace? Simple. Put a new lamb in the cage after the lion has eaten the previous one. Until it gets hungry again, it appears as if the lion and lamb are getting along. Hey, for some people, it only has to LOOK like peace.

Another not-so-funny joke is that someone wryly remarked, "It all depends on how you spell the word—p-e-a-c-e or p-i-e-c-e. They work in opposite ways, the former unifying the parts and the latter breaking them apart, but at least they SOUND the same. And many leaders who

---

[2] An acronym for "may his name and memory be erased."

have pressured Israel to surrender land for peace during the last several decades seem to have thought the two words were actually the same.

That is what people are sometimes forced to do when they lack *ohr haganuz*. Without it, the concept of peace doesn't really exist, just the letters *Shin* and *Mem*, which spell the word *shum*–there. When there is true harmony, the *ohr haganuz* must be present. Otherwise nothing is really there.

So where do we find *ohr haganuz*, which can make such a difference to our perspective, especially on world peace?

The answer is the subject of many very deep and kabbalistically detailed works from over the ages. You need to be able to access the *ohr haganuz* just to understand and properly relate to the words! Almost anyone can read them but, as the *Leshem* explained, it takes spiritually sensitive people to correctly process them.

However, a somewhat superficial discussion about the hidden light of Creation should be enough for now. The point can be made with the help of a simple analogy, and becomes even simpler with Google Maps.

Let's say you are looking for a specific location and type it into Google Maps. Usually within seconds the place is zeroed in on and located exactly. It is just a point on the map, identified by a virtual pin.

But there is an option to zoom out, which enlarges the area of the map as if you yourself were rising above the ground. As the range increases, the surrounding areas become part of the view. It is possible to see the location within the context of a much larger area, with the destination now in the context of more distant cities.

If you continue to fade back, the scope of the map increases, and can keep increasing until it covers the entire continent. Eventually the entire planet is visible. Google doesn't let you go any farther than that, so don't try looking at your destination from Jupiter or Saturn.

What good would that do anyhow? Physical locations on physical maps seen with physical eyes get too small to see long before then. By the time you see the entire country, the pin on the map may still be there but you won't be able to identify the location you asked about in the first place. That is a limitation of the physical world.

But not the spiritual world. The spiritual world, which is the basis of the physical world, doesn't have physical limitations—only spiritual ones. With physical eyes it is possible to see as far as a corner, but not around it. The mind's eye can see around corners beyond the physical world.

This is not about imagination, though it can play a role in this level of vision as well. We're talking about a mental picture that is constructed from actual knowledge, the level of which goes far beyond the rest of knowledge known to man. Man's understanding of Creation, as sophisticated as it is, is incredibly simple compared to this level of understanding.

In fact it is the difference between *Aitz Hada'as Tov v'Ra*, the Tree of Knowledge of Good and Evil—which is the basis of all secular knowledge—and *Aitz Hachaim*, the Tree of Life, which encompasses Torah on all four levels of *Pardes*.[3] The former is able to tell us HOW things work, but *Aitz Hachaim* tells us WHY they work that way.

Scientists and technologists are more concerned with the HOW, because it is necessary for harnessing Creation to improve the material quality of life. The philosopher is interested in the WHY because it answers nagging questions that once upon a time many people asked, especially "Why are we here?"

Today many people do not seem concerned with that question. There are just too many other things to think about, and life is so distracting that existentialism seems to be more a luxury than a necessity. Personal meaning and importance have shifted to more temporal values and goals.

However, there is a problem: What if there is a very specific purpose for why we're here, and we'll have to account for how well we fulfill it? What if there is eternal life and this world is truly just a corridor to get there, so we can earn sufficient merit to enter it? What if "what I don't know can't hurt me" isn't true at all?

This makes the WHY of life a much greater priority than the HOW. You can't just assume there isn't a WHY.

---

[3] Basically the Torah, *Mishnah*, Talmud, and Kabbalah.

That's incredibly irresponsible. You have to check it out first and see if the why does exist, because what you find meaningful enough to live for depends on it. Perhaps even the quality of your life right now.

Once you start to search for the why, you will be amazed at how far it goes—forever. It's not like secular knowledge, which has limits. The why, the reasoning behind everything, is God's knowledge, which is INFINITE. And the more of that knowledge you are able to access, the more you are able to increase your awareness of God's point of view, which is FAR more profound than anyone who hasn't accessed it can possibly imagine.

It sounds like hyperbole. Every believer wants to build up that which he believes in. But if you think about it, this is different. If this knowledge isn't man-made—which becomes self-evident early on—and it is truly God's sharing His vision of reality, then it has to be incredibly beyond any knowledge that man could come up with on his own.

We're smart, but not THAT smart.

We're godly, but not GOD.

Basically there are two ways to deal with any confusion over meaningful issues—either confront it directly or pretend it doesn't exist. If you try to tackle it and manage to make some sense from the encounter, then you will be able to work with it to the best of your ability. But if you can't, then you will be forced to persevere as long as you can until you have no choice but to work around the confusion as if it doesn't exist.

Even people who learn Torah do the same thing when reality becomes more complicated than their level of learning. But at least they have a direction, because the answers DO exist, just on a higher plane of learning. If people go far enough in their learning, they can reach a point where reality just can't faze them anymore.

Even if they can't make sense of EVERYTHING, they can at least make sense of ENOUGH to give them a sense of resolution beyond their grasp. The amount of *ohr haganuz* they have so far accessed may not be as intellectually clear to them as they would hope, but with it they can intuit beyond their grasp.

Very few people have such intellectual vision and clarity, which is why the *Lamed-Vav* of *shalom* is virtually absent. The world at large is certainly very distant from it for the time being. We need *Moshiach* to come to rid the world of the spiritual barriers that block mankind from being able to access the light of "peace" and leave behind the darkness of "piece" forever.

But as the Talmud alludes to and the *Leshem* explains, that doesn't mean that individuals in the meantime can't achieve peace—or at least some of it—for themselves. They just need to spiritually refine themselves and pursue the light. Then it will surely find them, and they will have a view of life that is literally out of this world.

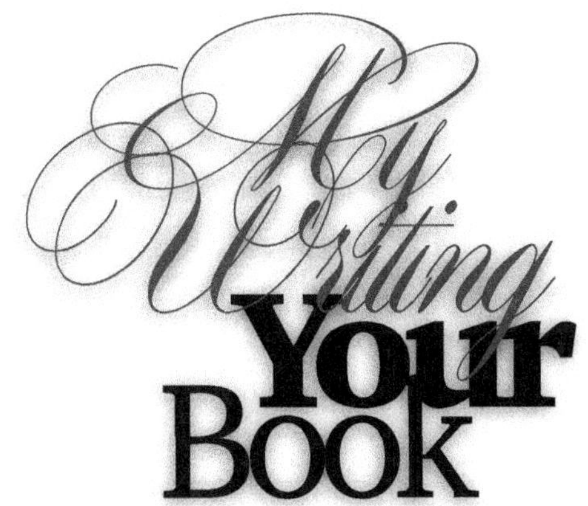

Chapter Nine. *Technology*

TECHNOLOGY IS GREAT, isn't it? It has made parts of life much more convenient and enjoyable. Most important of all, it has extended the abilities of many people, particularly the physically challenged. Technology has been an extremely valuable part of life, especially over the last 100 years.

But like many things, technology can be a blessing or a curse. If it allows people who are already trying to do their best to go beyond their limits to achieve more, it is a blessing. If it encourages people to get by with less effort, encouraging laziness and underachievement, then it is a curse. Shortcuts are beneficial only when they help us achieve meaningful accomplishments.

Kabbalah explains that *Adam Harishon*'s actual sin was that he didn't eat from *Aitz Hachaim* before eating from *Aitz Hada'as Tov v'Ra*. *Aitz Hachaim*, or Torah, would have taught him how to manage the knowledge of *Aitz Hada'as* in a wise and meaningful way.

Instead he ate from the Tree of Knowledge of Good and Evil without the wisdom of Torah required to prevent his newly inducted *yetzer hara*[1] from using technology to enhance material gain while reducing spiritual growth. He got ahead all right, just in the wrong direction.

To appreciate all this, it is necessary to know more about the background of life. People lead their daily lives under the impression that they are in total control, although they are being manipulated by all kinds of forces behind the scenes. People likewise go about their spiritual lives with the same mistaken impression. They become unwitting manipulated victims of a behind-the-scenes program.

The Talmud says that a person's *yetzer hara* rises every day to kill him, and that if God didn't intervene, it would succeed.[2] Even people who believe in such a concept usually think it is only minimally dangerous. Perhaps it causes people to be naughty from time to time, but not much more than that. They surely don't think it's treacherous enough to lead to suicide.

---

[1] Evil inclination.

[2] *Kiddushin* 30b.

People who wolf down fast food on a regular basis don't think they are harming themselves much or at all, nor do children who feed a candy addiction worry about the consequences. Is that because they know better? Or rather that they don't know enough.

Our goals are what define our path in life. The clearer we are about our objectives, the clearer we will be about our priorities. Success is definitely not random, but is rather the result of optimizing opportunities. Successful people are usually those who make a point of determining the prospects of success and how best to use them.

Some people prefer to live life one day at a time. Their philosophy is that they will know what they should do when the time comes, so why worry in advance? You can't live in the future and should not live in the past. You have to live in the moment, and that is exactly what they try to do.

There is wisdom in that idea, but not to the extent that such people think. Unquestionably there are times when it is to our advantage to think only about what is occurring at the moment, or we will miss out and later regret not having paid attention when we could have.

But there are other times when it is prudent to consider the past and be concerned about the future. Not doing that when it is appropriate will also cause regret later.

For example one of the most significant questions we can ask is whether there is a purpose to life and, if the answer is yes, what it is. If we're here for a specific reason, wouldn't it be a waste to die having ignored it, especially if what follows depends on our having fulfilled it?

Even after we discover the purpose of life, we must constantly review it. As we learn more, our comprehension and appreciation can increase, perhaps indicating a need to tweak our personal program.

Reviewing the purpose of life is also essential because it is easy to get pulled off track without even knowing it. Life is not a four-year course with specific goals that we're reminded of almost every day near exam times. Though college can be very distracting, most students are there for the same reason and are trying to reach the same or similar goals.

Not so life. Life can last 90-plus years and it has many different stages that involve many different people. In the course of that time the world can change dramatically, causing lives to unexpectedly do so as well. What's more problematic is that not everyone is on the same page and people can go in completely opposite directions, which often leads to violent confrontation.

To make matters worse, many people are striving to get ahead in life at the cost of our progress. We are also at the mercy of people who CLAIM to have our best interests at heart, but either don't or are wrong about what is truly in our best interest. Life can make us feel as if we are running across a no-man's land while being shot at from all sides.

Except for one main difference. At least in a military

no-man's land, the danger is clear and apparent. You know where it is and this makes it possible to at least try to avoid the risk. The no-man's land of life can be even more hazardous We can be failing at personal fulfillment while seemingly taking a walk in the park.

This war is different. The enemy is among us—actually inside us. That makes it FAR more difficult to distinguish between friend and foe. Like the terrorist the *yetzer hara* is, it does nothing but conspire all day long to bring us down by whatever means will work.

Its methods vary from generation to generation. It has to work with what is at its disposal, which amounts to whatever gets the most attention from us. Certainly in the last few decades a major focus has been technology. Notice how much time people spend on smartphones, and how much money they have poured into new equipment they may never use and certainly don't need.

It's like a magic show. A good magician knows how to keep his audience looking in one direction so he can do a trick in another without anyone noticing what he is actually doing. Only the results are apparent, and they appear to be truly magical.

That's all well and good when it comes to entertainment. We WANT to be fooled. We WANT the joke to be on us and are even willing to pay for it. But not when it comes to life. At some point before we die, we're going to look back and wonder about many of the investments we made, and what we were thinking at the time. We may not figure out exactly how the *yetzer hara* did us in on many occasions, but we'll definitely know that it did.

No regrets? For now. While we still have a *yetzer hara*, we lack the ability to be sure about what we need to be clear about. At least on our own. If we develop a desire to know truth, then God will help us see through the machinations of the *yetzer hara* and get back on track while there is still time to make amends.

That's like eating from *Aitz Hachaim*. Turning to God and learning Torah are paths to the wisdom necessary to bridle the knowledge of *Aitz Hada'as*. That is when technology stops being a distracting and major stumbling block and begins to fulfill its vital function of extending our abilities for good.

In fact it has been very helpful for teaching Torah and contributing to our understanding of profound and abstract concepts. Long before technology was a household word, Kabbalah spoke about theoretical concepts often difficult to grasp. It is hard to conceive of something that goes beyond human experience.

The physical world is the way it is because of the spiritual world. Whatever happens in the physical world and how it happens is due to its reflection of the spiritual world. Therefore lessons about the invisible world can be derived from the physical world. They help us learn about the spiritual world that we cannot see. The more abstract our understanding of the physical world becomes, the more this holds true.

Take the idea of the *sefiros* for example. They are a central part of the discussion of Creation from a kabbalistic point of view. They are completely spiritual entities that God created to transmit His infinite light and implement His will, which is what directs all history.

The system of *sefiros* is extremely complex and abstract, and for the longest time was probably beyond the intellectual reach of many who tried to understand it. There wasn't much in everyday life to use as a comparison to help grasp how the *sefiros* work.

Until man discovered electricity. It wasn't the result of a mystical search or drive to recognize the kabbalistic roots of Creation. It was something in nature that caught the attention of the inquisitive minds of some people who set out to understand and eventually master it. After years of research and experimentation, the technology was created to supply entire cities with this natural wonder.

Once a large amount of electricity could be generated, the next step was to figure out how to safely deliver it to its destination. Too much can burn its cables and blow up power stations. Too little means that locations farther away from the source won't get enough electricity for their needs.

Eventually the developers created methods to reduce the electrical flow in stages so that it could be as strong as needed to travel the full intended distance and also weak enough to be safe to use. Over time the procedure became so advanced that now it can be regulated on demand, even automatically.

The *sefiros* work similarly. God's light is too intense at its source for Creation to exist, let alone function. Since Creation was made for man to use free will and choose to follow the Creator or not, it has to be possible for us to reject God and even doubt His existence while He is maintaining the entire world.

Just the creation of the various aspects of the universe, both physical and spiritual, requires the light of God to be specifically adjusted in order to allow one thing to exist differently from another. With countless combinations of *sefiros* and levels of divine light, the variation is too fantastic for us to even begin to fathom, especially since the physical and spiritual are made from the same material.

The *sefiros* regulate everything according to the will of God. Like transformers, they receive one level of light, holding back some of it while allowing the remainder to continue on, creating or maintaining what it must for the sake of history. And that literally varies every moment on many different levels in ways we can't possibly comprehend—which indicates just how much more sophisticated God's system is than our electrical one.

Nevertheless technology does help us understand some of the abstractness of Kabbalah. And as science probes deeper into the very fabric of Creation, new insights constantly emerge that provide more approaches to explain the goings-on of the mysterious spiritual world.

That is one crucial but rarely appreciated aspect of technology. The part that people seem to value more readily is how it can be used to further the cause of Torah. Just look how much Torah outreach has been done since organizations put up their own websites. Note how many Torah sources can be studied online at no cost, and how quickly a resource can be found.

There is no question that the Torah world has benefited from scientific advancements, allowing for better organization and utilization of resources. Fundraising has definitely profited from technology, as well as the business of publishing and selling *seforim*.[3] Making *Shabbos* is easier and more fun now that technology has entered the *shomer Shabbos*[4] kitchen.

From the simple reading of the Torah, the knowledge of *Aitz Hada'as* was off limits, and it seemed as if it would always be like that. Kabbalah explains otherwise, and says that had *Adam Harishon* waited until *Shabbos* before eating, the two trees would have merged and become one, the complete *Aitz Chaim*. This was what God intended to happen from the beginning.

It's taken thousands of years, but over the last century the trees have finally seemed to be uniting, especially in more recent times as the Torah world finds fitting ways to benefit from secular advancement. There have been some

---

[3] Plural of *sefer*—book.
[4] Observant of the Sabbath.

amazing successes as well as tragic failures. The merging of technology and Torah is far from perfect, leading to questions of whether the benefit is worth the risk.

Unfortunately the answer to that question is not always available at the start. The results are frequently not known until after damage has occurred, or a squandered opportunity becomes known to those who lost it. There is nothing wrong with profiting from secular achievements if managed properly. But many people carry too big a *yetzer hara* and not enough *seichel*,[5] so the result is sin, distraction, or *bittul Torah*.[6]

People who decided to try to make the best of both worlds need to learn from the mistakes of the past, particularly those of *Adam Harishon*. Before eating from any aspect of *Aitz Hada'as*, they need to make sure they have sated themselves with the wisdom of *Aitz Hachaim*. Then clarity of purpose and fear of God will protect them.

---

[5] Intelligence.

[6] Although *bittul* means to cancel something, such as an appointment, it can also mean to waste something, time for example. Instead of using time for Torah study, it is rather spent on something less important. Thus *bittul Torah* means neglect of Torah study.

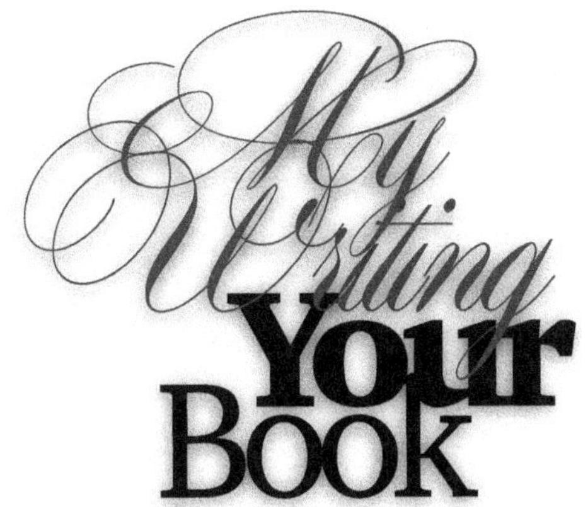

Your Book

Chapter Ten. Entertainment

ENTERTAINMENT IS ONE of those things that just seem to be part and parcel of life. People, every last one of us, NEED to be entertained by what we are doing or we become bored and sometimes despondent. The more entertained we are at any moment, the more we will be IN the moment, and that is where life is lived.

The only variable from society to society—and it is a crucial one—is the form the entertainment takes. The type of entertainment that talks to a society tells a lot about that society and its values. At the end of the day this can determine whether its people will be going up or down[1]

---

[1] That is, to either heaven or hell (*gihenom*).

when all is said and done.

Each form of entertainment can be placed on a single continuum. To the right of center would be those that are spiritually entertaining and to the left would be physical kinds of entertainment. The more extreme the form of entertainment, the more to the right or left of center it will be.

It seems to be that the more spiritual people are, the less physical entertainment they require to be content. Spiritual people tend to feel very much alive without superficial entertainment, and are repulsed by its cruder forms. They don't need to be shocked or risk death in order to appreciate life.

Not being physical, spiritual entertainment can often be self-generated on demand. Physical entertainment on the other hand usually requires planning and some form of external activity to access it. This has made a lot of entertainment providers VERY rich.

Even though entertainment is such a common part of everyday life, few people really understand what it is. In a sense it is like medicine—we know we need it, and although we have little or no idea of how it works, we are usually willing to trust the suppliers that it is what we require.

How much damage has been caused by medication meant to help people? A scary amount. Likewise, how much damage is occurring to society because of both the amount and kind of entertainment people are subjected to? An even scarier amount.

The good news is that there ARE alternative forms of medicine, which not only help but also don't harm. Since they don't have many of the dangerous side effects of synthetic pharmaceutical products, more and more people are turning to them.

Likewise there are alternative forms of entertainment with only positive side effects. But to appreciate them we have to first understand what entertainment is.

So what IS entertainment?

Before we can address that question it is necessary to mention that people are composed of two parts, body and soul. Although both the body AND the soul live for pleasure, the soul's idea of a good time is a positive SPIRITUAL experience. Ultimately this does something to enhance our capacity to infuse life with additional meaning.

The body likes pleasurable physical sensations. Certain activities make it feel better, while others cause it pain. It will therefore pursue the former and avoid the latter, even though doing so may ultimately deny it the opportunity to fulfill significant goals.

Whenever the body has to do something uncomfortable, it will likely be done only because the result is expected to be pleasurable. For example, getting up early in the morning to work out is a hard sell for a body. But if doing so leads to better health or some kind of competitive success, the body will go along with it. Adding some favorite music during a workout might even encourage it to look forward to the workout.

Getting a body to agree to rise early to learn Torah before *dovening*[2] is a more difficult proposition for a body. The soul will be all for it but the body will probably say, "Leave me alone. Why aren't you happy that I let you get up on time for *dovening?*" Spiritual activities, especially at the cost of physical comforts, just don't cut it for the body.

But how about a freshly brewed cup of coffee while you learn?

When I was living in Toronto, I used to *doven*[3] at a *shul*[4] that always provided coffee in the morning. The first one to arrive would start the coffee machine, and everyone else was greeted with the enticing aroma of freshly brewed coffee.

I already had enough reasons to get to *shul* early to learn, but the coffee certainly made my drive on dark and cold winter mornings more bearable. Just knowing that there was good coffee waiting, my body seemed to say, "Can't you drive any faster?"

The learning entertained my soul.

The coffee entertained my body.

It's not a secret, but it is also not an idea that is appreciated enough. You have to figure out how to get to your body—to find something in spiritual pleasures that

---

[2] Praying.

[3] Pray.

[4] Synagogue.

interests your body as well. That's the challenge in life. That is actually the challenge OF life, and the person who can meet that test dies only in this world to live forever in the next one.

Unfortunately for many it has worked the other way around. They have been challenged to convince their souls that they will gain from the fulfillment of the whims of their bodies. Obviously not true, but people who are losing the battle to their bodies aren't inclined to see that.

Since the very beginning of time, physical pleasures have been the most tantalizing. They're right there in the open, and they speak to the body really well. *Chava* sinned and ate from *Aitz Hada'as*, the Tree of Knowledge, only because it appealed to her eyes; she overlooked the Tree of Life because it didn't.[5]

The wisest man who ever lived, *Shlomo Hamelech*, explained:

> It is a tree of life for those who GRASP it. (*Mishlei* 3:18)

Torah is a tree of life no matter what. But it can only become a tree of life for people who GRASP it. They have to CHOOSE to give it a serious look, some very serious consideration, and then take the time to know what it is

---

[5] According to the *Ohr Hachaim*, the bark of the Tree of Life was its fruit, something that did not catch the body's attention so readily.

and what it can do for them. Few people have turned away from Torah after honestly doing that.

This perhaps scares a lot of bodies. They may already sense that Torah is a one-way ticket if it is learned properly, and therefore fear its impositions and restrictions. Not having grasped Torah, the body cannot possibly see what benefit it offers. So how could it possibly be happy living by Torah?

That is the soul's job. Does an adolescent who wants to skip school and play or sleep all day appreciate that he or she will one day want to do just the opposite to get ahead in life? Of course not. It is something that has to be discovered and appreciated over time.

It is the same for the body. Can a body that is born quite physical and hasn't yet experienced the pleasures of spiritual greatness give up short-term fun for long-term reward? Of course not. It is something that has to be taught and only then will the body appreciate that it has a lot more in common with the soul than it previously assumed.

This is what *ba'alei teshuvah* find. When they were secular, they shunned a religious lifestyle. But after adequate exposure to the logic and values of Torah, they embrace it and WILLINGLY relinquish diversions once believed to be indispensable to their happiness. After first grasping Torah spiritually, they begin to do so physically as well.

It doesn't mean that *ba'alei teshuvah* no longer enjoy tasty food or fine conversation. If anything, they like them even more, because they fit into a meaningful context, like *Shabbos* for example. Dressing well, within reason, is a *kiddush Hashem*, a sanctification of God's Name. Exercise under the right conditions is a Torah *mitzvah* since you are taking care of the body God gave you, which you need to serve Him.

Indeed, the *ba'al teshuvah* may still love that fresh cup of coffee, perhaps even with a piece of cake. As the soul is nourished and enthralled by Torah learning, the body is savoring the delicious food accompanying the experience. The person learns and becomes wiser, and both soul AND body benefit from the additional personal greatness achieved.

If people understand and continue down this path, then even the cake and coffee become unnecessary. Many people are completely unaware that their bodies have a lot more spiritual potential than it might appear. Consider how many children, who exhibited little greatness when they were young, grew up to become great successes.

The *Midrash* teaches that when it came time for *Moshe Rabbeinu* to die, the Angel of Death had a difficult time fetching his soul. Apparently *Moshe*'s body had become so much like his soul that it refused to let go of the soul, despite the fact that heaven waited for it. God had to come and take it Himself.

The expression is "when in Rome, do as the Romans do." But this is not always the best advice. If we stand back and take a hard look at the world, it certainly seems like a body's world, and the vast majority of forms of entertainment are designed to satisfy its most base instincts.

In this case doing as the Romans do means stifling the soul while leaving the body to live unaccomplished, not fulfilling its potential. People will have little or nothing to show for their time here on earth, and will certainly lack the price of admission to the next world. It would definitely be advisable to not do as the Romans do but rather as the soul says, so that life will truly be entertaining the way God meant it to be. This will become clearer in the next chapter about free will.

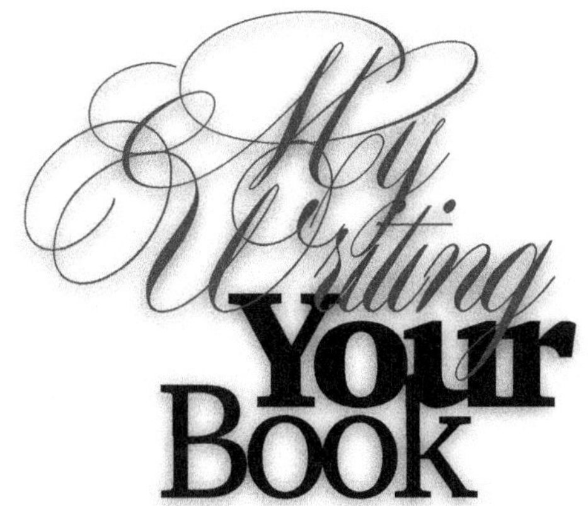

Chapter Eleven. *Free Will*

DO WE HAVE free will? This issue has been hotly debated for thousands of years, at least among people who care about it. The vast majority of people get uptight when they are denied the opportunity to do what they choose to do. Whether or not God knows the future or what that might mean in terms of actual free will doesn't concern them.

If God does know the future though, doesn't that mean we don't have free will? The short answer is that it really doesn't matter. If God says that we have free will and we will be judged on how we use it, that should be good enough for us. You can argue with God all you want about the philosophical issues regarding the whole concept of free will, but in the end He will tell you, "As far as I am concerned, you had free will and that is what your judgement will be based on!"

People may try to tell you that God, being omniscient, knows the future even before it occurs. From His perspective we have already made choices that we still don't know we're going to make. If so, how can our will be free?

That is not a valid question. When we make a decision based on how we choose to deal with our current set of circumstance, it is called choice. External factors that may have entered the picture to manipulate our decision don't matter at all. In the end it is still our decision because it is OUR chosen response to a situation as we perceive it.

Yes, it is true that we are the product of many things we never had a say about, such as family, upbringing, schools, teachers, and people we met along the way. We are exposed to things by surprise, which influence us in ways we would rather have avoided. How much of who we are is really what WE choose to be?

If someone were giving out money and gave $100 to one person and gave you only $20, you could argue about the unfairness of it and mope about the inequality of your situation. But at the end of the day you still have only $20. The question you will be asked is what you did with that $20.

You won't be asked what you might have done had you been given $100. The only consideration is what you

DID do compared to what you COULD have done with what you were given. THAT is what shows what was important to you—how you looked at life, how you thought…what you made of YOURSELF.

The best moral choice for someone might be between great and only good. He might have had a chance to do something outstanding, albeit with self-sacrifice, or just do it on a lower level. For example, he could give $200 for *tzedakah* or half that amount, leaving him with less money with which to enjoy life.

He could say, "At least I helped out. $100 is a lot of money for me." But when he later sees what the extra $100 would have brought in terms of ETERNAL reward versus the temporal pleasure it provided in this world, he will wonder, "What was I thinking?" *Mesiras nefesh*—self-sacrifice for *mitzvos* is the currency of the World-to-Come, not the money we earn and spend in this world.

The best moral choice for others might be stealing $50 instead of $100. The nature of their soul together with everything they were exposed to might make stealing or another sin almost inevitable . But they too have a conscience, and can use it to at least minimalize the extent of their infractions. That is their response to what they were given, and the issues they were presented with.

Our personal capacity for moral choice basically comes down to two factors: our intrinsic nature and personal *yetzer hara*. Our soul has an intrinsic nature that heavily influences us. That is what makes some of us naturally laid back and others naturally uptight. Upbringing obviously plays a role, but usually not as much as intrinsic nature.

Even our body type has much to say about how we turn out. How we look to ourself and the functioning of our body affect our self-confidence and level of laziness among other things. We are also greatly impacted by how others perceive and respond to us—with kindness or a lack thereof—which in turn affects how we treat ourself.

Then there is our *yetzer hara*, the evil inclination. What is it really? It's…it's…you know , that thing in all of us that makes us do something naughty, especially when we know the right way to behave. The frightening thing is how it does that to so many people at one time, which compels God to reboot history, completely or partially.

But what exactly is the *yetzer hara*?

That's harder to explain. The answer is kabbalistic and has to do with the *klipos*.[1] These entities existed long before man was created, and were created specifically in order to actualize evil so that mankind could have free will. Although the *klipos* are completely spiritual, they tend to affect us physically and cause our body to respond to circumstances in self-serving ways that do NOT bring us closer to God.

---

[1] Literally peels, because they block a person from spirituality. Anything that spiritually desensitizes a person, in whatever form it takes, is a function of the *klipos*.

The evidence of that might be something as basic as an instinctual response at a time that we need to rise above instinct and act nobly. We may be hungry and want to eat an entire sandwich. But something inside us, the *yetzer tov*—good inclination—compels us to share it, and love someone else as we love ourself. The inner conflict is the reason for life. The resolution of it determines who we are and ultimately where we go after this world is over.

The *yetzer hara*'s manipulation is far more obvious when the need isn't a matter of survival but rather of desire. The *yetzer hara* tries to turn it into a matter of survival in order to achieve its goal. But not every lack we feel needs to be filled to enable us to carry on with our life. Many wants are only momentary, and passing them up, as heroic as it may be, in no way interferes with what we need to do or become.

Anyone who has dieted in one way or another, for one reason or another, recognizes this. It might be an issue of calorie reduction for health purposes, minimizing alcohol consumption to avoid worsening a liver condition, or refraining from dangerous driving. It might be a people diet—avoiding certain people to remove the danger of speaking *loshon hara*.[2] No matter what the circumstances, people will feel compelled to bend or break the rules to do something wrong, and afterward feel terrible and re-

---

[2] Derogatory speech about someone, a serious offence by Torah standards.

gretful.

At the very beginning the *yetzer hara* was easier to recognize. It was outside man in the form of a snake, so it used its own brain, its own mouth, and clearly spoke its own mind. It successfully tripped up mankind, but when it came to meting out punishment, the snake was singled out for its role in the downfall of mankind and Creation.

It's a long kabbalistic story, but matters got worse after that, not better. Instead of learning from our mistake and going our separate way, the *yetzer hara* joined with us, actually moving in. Now it was just a question of time until it worked its way to the top and began to act like the boss.[3]

One reason it gets away with that is because it speaks through OUR brain, and we hear ITS thoughts just as we hear our own. People uneducated in the nuances of the *yetzer hara* think they are hearing their OWN thoughts, not those of the *yetzer hara*. Tragically many end up capitulating to those thoughts as if they were their own will, often with very destructive results.

This has given rise to a lucrative profession which helps people differentiate between the thoughts that are their own and those that aren't—so that they can take charge of their lives and live more meaningfully. This situation can be compared to moving next door to a criminal without being notified in advance, leaving you to suffer the

---

[3] *Sha'ar Hagilgulim*, Introduction 23.

consequences of a dangerous neighbor.

Society recognizes that the world consists of good people and evil people. Most people are aware of evil being out there, and perhaps that they themselves are capable of contributing to it. But for the most part they look at evil people as belonging to a different species from the one they belong to. They don't understand that the people doing recognizable evil are the same as they are, but perhaps more extreme.

Who in the secular world is aware of the *yetzer hara* with which everyone is born? It's there from before birth, with our good inclination kicking in only at age 12 for a girl and 13 for a boy. It gets a real head start, making life the uphill moral battle it is and is meant to be.

As God told *Kayin*:

> If you do not improve, however, sin is lying at the entrance and to you is its longing, but you can rule over it.[4]

How many people are aware of this, let alone think about it and take it to heart? Even a Torah-observant Jew doesn't always notice when he is being played on by his *yetzer hara*, or the seriousness of allowing it to have its way. Often it's not until we recite the confessional prayer on *Yom Kippur* that we finally take to heart the numerous

---

[4] *Bereishis* 4:7.

battle scars we wear.

The scars can be small or large. Just ask yourself how many spiritual transgressions you committed yesterday. Then again, if you don't realize what you should have done instead, you probably won't recognize that what you did was lacking in any way.

There is a story of a fisherman returning from a successful fishing trip who met *Eliyahu* the prophet, and did not identify him. The fisherman seemed joyful, and the prophet inquired about his reason for his happiness.

"We're not always successful when we go out to fish," he replied, "but today we were very successful, thank God."

"Wonderful," *Eliyahu* told him. "And what about your Torah learning?"

Caught off guard, the fisherman paused and then answered, "Unfortunately I was not blessed with the ability to learn Torah."

"I see," said *Eliyahu*. "But you were clearly blessed to know how to fish!"

"Oh yes," said the fisherman said with pride. "God has blessed me with the ability to learn all the intricacies of my trade. That is the reason for my success!"

"Very true," *Eliyahu* agreed, but then he continued and said, "Tell me, don't you think God, Who blessed you to be a wise fisherman, would also bless you to learn the Torah He holds so dear?"

The smile on the fisherman's face disappeared. That

hadn't occurred to him. He just assumed that since fishing came so easily to him, that was what God wanted him to do. Learning Torah was difficult, so rather than struggle, he instead focused on fishing only. It didn't occur to him that God would mind. He was beginning to see his mistake, and tears welled up in his eyes.

Eliyahu noticed that the fisherman had taken his point to heart and was changing his mind, so he consoled him, "You aren't alone in this. Like you, many others have pursued their material life over one of Torah because that was easier for them. At least you are finding out now, while you can still turn things around. Many others won't find out until their day of judgment, when it will be too late to fix anything."

What we don't know won't hurt us?

Untrue. Just ask any *ba'al teshuvah*, someone who took the time to find out what he had not previously known about God, Torah, and life. The new information opened his eyes and mind to what he was overlooking, and how things he thought God did not mind actually made a BIG difference to Him. Like so many others, he assumed that God's patience meant He either wasn't there or didn't care.

Learning Torah changes all that for *ba'alei teshuvah*. They no longer take their actions for granted. They discovered the purpose of life and what they were capable of being, what they were EXPECTED to be. And that is precisely when their *yetzer hara* really kicked in. The more they tried to align themselves with the will of God, the more they felt it confronting them, and suddenly free will became more REAL.

For them, but not for many billions of people who do not know what a *yetzer hara* is or how it works. For them, but not for the countless others who think that the purpose of life is just to make it to the age of 90 and have a good time doing so. For them, and not for people throughout the ages who lived with the idea that there is no World-to-Come, and who therefore invested all their marbles in this period of history.

Do we have free will? You decide. But before you do, make sure you have all the necessary facts. The *yetzer hara* takes advantage of us when we don't. It can never make a decision for us, or we wouldn't be culpable for our sins. But it surely can make it easy as pie for us to decide to sin, by distracting us from truth so that we do not know we are choosing a lie.

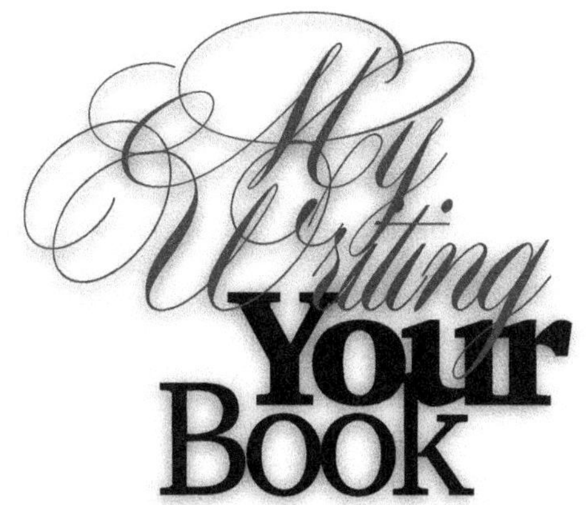

Chapter Twelve. *Honesty*

ONE LAST CHAPTER for now, honestly. It's about honesty, something we would prefer not to have to write about but it's unfortunately necessary. As the Talmud states, one of the signs that *Moshiach* is not far off is that truth will be scarce.[1] He must be verrrrrrry close.

Someone might ask, "If God Himself changes the truth, as Rashi points out at the beginning of *Parashas Vayaira*, then why can't we?" This question indicates that the person is already in trouble. First of all, he is comparing himself to God—and that itself is troubling. Second, he is looking for justification to be untruthful, and that may be

---

[1] *Sanhedrin* 97a.

more troubling.

Why is it so important to be honest?

There are many reasons, some more significant than others. To begin with, reality is like a puzzle and every piece has its place. If you force a piece into the wrong place, even if it is a close fit, the puzzle is ruined and the damage will affect other pieces as well.

Reality, however, is different from a puzzle inasmuch as it will seem to correct itself at some point. God made Creation for a very specific reason, and He won't accept second best in response. One way or another, He makes sure that whatever has gone wrong is righted at some point—and that usually has dramatically painful consequences for man.

Just consider *Noach* and his generation.

Just ask all the sufferers of war.

Lies have a way of coming back and haunting us, even when we can't recognize their effect. It's the God-built nature of reality.

That's on a global scale. Then there is the personal level. It's often hard not to lie, especially when under pressure. It's almost instinctual for some. The hard part is living with the lie afterward, after the crime has been committed and the body has calmed down enough to allow the soul to have its say.

The Torah tells us that we were made in the image of

God.[2] The Talmud tell us that the seal of God is truth.[3] Combining both statements, we see that we were created to be honest, although we were also created with the capacity to be dishonest. You can call it conscience that shames us for bending the truth, but it is really just our essential nature kicking in and reminding us how uncomfortable it is to go against it.

If you don't believe in any of this, you might be inclined to say that what people call conscience is really just the result of religious indoctrination. Early notions of right and wrong that grew out of the biblical era were absorbed by society until they became part of man's consciousness.

The proponents of this opinion not only say that there is nothing wrong with changing this view, they argue that it is healthier to do so. Why should people in today's world be held back from doing what comes naturally because of what some socially underdeveloped societies wrongly felt was inappropriate?

If you agree with that point of view, you have a friend in Adolf Hitler, *ysv'z*. One of his major justifications for eliminating every last Jew was the moral conscience HE believed THEY imposed on mankind. As a social darwinist he believed in survival of the fittest and not lending a helping hand to the weak in need.

---

[2] *Bereishis* 1:26. The Talmud says that an angel teaches a Jew all of Torah before birth, so the truth is already inside us (*Niddah* 30b).
[3] *Yoma* 69b.

He certainly did not believe in the Torah's claim that man was made in the image of God. He believed that man should be made in the image of the Aryan race, blond, blue-eyed, etc. The Greeks had their idea of human perfection, sculpted it, and put personifications of it into the Olympics. The Romans adopted the ideal and then adapted it to their liking, as did the Catholic Church. Renaissance artists went to great pains to do the same, until the Nazis eventually came along and imposed their version of human perfection on as much of the world as they could reach.

It is not coincidence that every version of human perfection has led to one tragedy or another. Most models were based on physical traits and abilities, which have less to say about a person than the soul inside. Only the soul, a piece of divine light, can compel someone to be LIKE God, especially when the body is pulling in the opposite direction.

Owning up to this idea in general is the basis of honesty. Owning up to it personally is the basis of SELF-honesty. It obligates us to figure out the moral path in any given situation and then to take it. It may be easier to do this when alone, but it is equally important when with others, especially when those others reject the moral response and even ridicule those who follow it.

Shakespeare had Macbeth say, "To thine own self be true." The first meaning is that someone has to determine as best he can whether he has done what he should or could have done. The second meaning is that one must be honest in his ways and relationships. The third meaning is that one must always do the right thing.[4]

This advice was great for the ages. Did Shakespeare himself follow it? Have countless others who read or watched the play? They may have tried, but in order to succeed we have to know what the right thing is. First we must understand what truth really is because, as we learn from God at the beginning of *Parashas Vayaira*, it doesn't always mean conveying the facts as they happened.

After all, it was *Ya'akov Avinu*, the MAN OF TRUTH, who masqueraded as his brother to deceive his father into giving him blessings meant for *Eisav*. True, it was his mother, *Rivkah*, who commanded him to do it, but *Ya'akov* was certainly old enough to say no. As the Talmud states, you only have to honor your parents' wishes to the point they don't contradict God's.[5]

Ya'akov never rebutted what his mother was asking him to do by saying it was morally corrupt. He argued only that it was risky because should he be caught, which was likely, he would end up being cursed by his father rather than blessed.[6] Nor did *Ya'akov* point out that a blessing can only go to the person intended by the one giving it. Those issues never came up, at least not in the Torah.

---

[4] Https://literarydevices.net/to-thine-own-self-be-true/.
[5] *Yevamos* 5b.
[6] *Bereishis* 27:12.

The Talmud reports that when *Ya'akov* fled *Eisav* after successfully taking the latter's blessings and ending up far away at his Uncle Lavan's house, he seemingly bragged about his newfound ability to be tricky. When Rachel warned *Ya'akov* about her father's scheming ways, *Ya'akov* called himself his "brother in trickery."[7]

Normally this kind of behavioral change means that someone has lost his moral compass along the way. He has gone off the *derech*, which means he has left the way of Torah for a dubious way of life. As many an offender has confessed, it's the first offense that is most difficult to commit. After that it just keeps getting easier. The Talmud concurs.[8]

But that's not what happened to *Ya'akov Avinu*. He wasn't called the man of truth solely because he used to like to tell the truth. Truth was part and parcel of his intrinsic nature, right down to his soul. His trait was *Tifferes*, the spiritual origin of the written Torah—not to mention the soul of *Moshe Rabbeinu* .

Ya'akov never deviated from the truth.

Truth compelled him to act as he did.

Because let's face it, life after the sin of *Adam Harishon* became very different from what it was previously. Before the sin man only perceived truth and falsehood.

---

[7] *Megillah* 13b.

[8] *Kiddushin* 20a: If a person sins once, twice, three times, it become permissible to him—that is, as if it is permissible to him.

After sinning and suffering from intellectual and spiritual confusion, people were downgraded to see good and evil instead. Since then history has shown people's mistaken ideas of both.

That's why God gave man His Torah, against the advice[9] of the angels. He shouldn't have had to do that. Since the Torah was the blueprint for Creation,[10] man should have been able to figure out truth and falsehood from the world as it was created, just as *Avraham* had done.

But people didn't, and they still don't. So God decided to share the blueprint with them, to show what they so carelessly overlooked while living in the world. He might have done it earlier if someone had been here to receive it. It took an *Avraham*, three generations of descendants, and 116 years of slavery to develop people who were capable of accepting it.

Unlike other blueprints, the Torah contains a lot more information than it seems it should. Every building plan comes with a book of specifications, the myriad details necessary to enable the builder to accurately actualize the blueprint he is following. There are forces at work to undermine the integrity of the construction, and the book of specs is provided to plug as many holes as possible.

In Torah terms the Written Law, the five books of *Moshe*, is the blueprint. The Oral Law is the book of specs,

---

[9] *Shabbos* 88b.
[10] *Bereishis* Rabbah 1:1.

which essentially contains the *Mishnah*, Talmud, and countless commentaries added over the years to help Jews get it right from GOD'S point of view.

But it doesn't stop there. These two massive bodies of Torah knowledge—the word of God—are enough to help a Jew properly execute *mitzvos* and avoid sin. They are his ticket to the World-to-Come as well as to receiving a good portion in it. But they really cover only three levels of Torah learning—*Pshat*, *Remez*, and *Drush,* Simple, Hint, and Exegesis. There is a fourth.

Called *Sod*—Secret, it refers to Jewish mysticism, Kabbalah. Kabbalah is basically God saying to man, "Do you want to know why and how I made Creation they way I did? Here. Learn this. It'll blow your mind."

Someone may ask, "Why do I need my mind blown? What if I am content just knowing what is revealed already? Since I now have enough material to learn over several lifetimes, much of which is essential for properly living by *halachah*, why should I complicate matters by going into the why of it all?"

This is a valid question with a valid answer, which a story will help provide.

A rabbi of a *shul* happened to pass the local train station when he spied his trusted *gabbai* eating in a *treif* restaurant! Horrified, the rabbi continued on his way, trying to figure out how to deal with this situation.

Hours later the rabbi had calmed down enough to phone the *gabbai*. There was no answer. He tried again but still no answer. It wasn't until much later than night that he finally reached the *gabbai*'s wife, who told him that her husband was in the hospital.

The rabbi certainly wasn't going to confront his soon to be ex-*gabbai* during his recovery in the hospital. But it put him in an awkward position. People would expect him to pay a visit to this fellow *shul* member and until they learned the truth, they surely wouldn't understand why he didn't. He would have to go, he reasoned to himself, and pretend that he knew nothing about the sin until the appropriate time came along to confront the phony.

So the next day the rabbi hesitatingly and begrudgingly showed up at the room of the *gabbai*. He had decided to stay only a short while before excusing himself, lest he lose control and say things he didn't want to, at least not then. Entering the room, he was greeted with a huge smile and tremendous thanks, which made HIM feel like the dishonest one.

During that visit the rabbi learned one of his most important lessons ever. The *gabbai* told him about the ailment that had forced him to the hospital, a bleeding ulcer, and added, "And you know the worst part of it? My ulcer started to bleed while I was at the train station. On my doctor's orders, I was forced to eat *treif* food to save myself from possible death. I still haven't recovered from THAT!" the *gabbai* said with a look of disgust.

The rabbi was of average height but at that moment he felt about two inches tall. He had forgotten about his trusted *gabbai*'s ulcer and the protocol of what to do if it started to bleed. "No wonder," he now thought to himself, "he ate as if he hadn't seen food for months!"

He had wrongly made one of the most honorable members of his community into one of the most dishonorable. What he heard made him feel both relieved, grateful, and horrible at the same time—relieved that he had been wrong, grateful that he didn't say anything about it, and horrible for not having judged the *gabbai* to the side of merit.

The smartest people have made terrible mistakes. As the wisest man of all, *Shlomo Hamelech*, said, "There is not a righteous man on earth who always does what is right and never sins."[11] He himself certainly sinned .

At the end of the day it is usually more a matter of what we do NOT know that leads us astray rather than what we DO know. It is one thing to know the truth and disregard it—in that case we at least know what the truth is, can feel ashamed for ignoring it, and possibly do *teshuvah* to make amends.

But it is something completely different to not even know what the truth is. We can be dishonest without being conscious of it. We have everything to feel guilty about but lack the awareness to know it. We can't do *teshuvah* because we don't even notice we have to. We're a lost cause, utterly dependent on the mercy of God.

---

[11] *Koheles* 7:20.

As one *chozer b'teshuvah* expressed it, at first he thought that he had done God a favor by becoming Torah observant. As he learned more, he decided that they had done each other a favor, he by becoming more observant and God by helping him find the truth.

As he continued to learn, he realized what he had almost passed up and how much spiritual damage he had brought about by his previous behavior. He realized that he had deserved worse than death and was amazed that God had allowed him to continue long enough to discover the truth and change in its direction.

He understood finally that the only favor being done for anyone is one that God does and did for him, granting him a second chance at life. And the more he learned, the more he appreciated that insight and thanked God for it. He had been granted the greatest gift one can receive in a lifetime: the opportunity to know truth and to live by it.

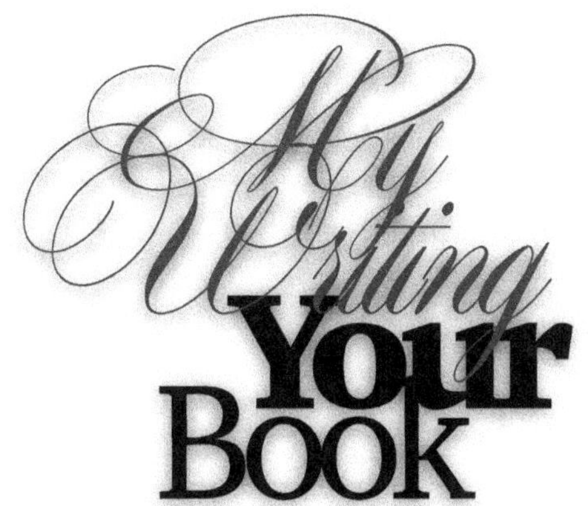

Other Books

THE FOLLOWING TITLES are all the books written over the years. Some books may no longer be in print, but many are still available in either PDF or Kindle formats. Visit the Thirtysix.org OnLine Bookstore, or Amazon for more information, or to order online.

The Unbroken Chain of Jewish Tradition, 1985
The Eternal Link, 1990
If Only I Were Wealthy, 1992
If Only I Understood Why, 1993
If Only I Could See the Forest, 1993
If Only I Could Stay, 1993
If Only Great Was Greater, 1993
The Y Factor, 1994

Life's A Thrill, 1994
No Atheists in a Foxhole, 1994
Changes that Last Forever, 1994
The Making of a Great Jewish Leader, 1994
Bereishis: A Beginning With No End, 1994
The Wonderful World of Thirtysix, 1995
Redemption to Redemption, 1997
The Big Picture, 1998
Perceptions, 1998
Not Just Another Scenario, 2001
At The Threshold, 2001
Anticipating Redemption, 2002
Sha'ar HaGilgulim, 2002
Hadran (Hebrew), 2004
Talking About The End of Days, 2005
Talking About Eretz Yisroel, 2005
The Physics of Kabbalah, 2006
Be Positive, 2007
Geulah b'Rachamim, 2007
God.calm, 2007
Just Passing Through, 2007
On The Same Page, 2007
The Equation of Life, 2007
No Such Victim, 2009
Survival in 10 Easy Steps, 2009
Not Just Another Scenario 2, 2011
All In Your Mind, 2011
The Light of Thirtysix, 2011
The Last Exile, 2011
Drowning in Pshat, 2012

Drown No More, 2012

Shas Man, 2013

The Mystery of Jewish History, 2013

Survival Guide For the End-of-Days, 2013

Deeper Perceptions, 2013

Chanukah Lite, 2015

The Hitchhiker's Guide to Armageddon, 2016

Purim Lite, 2016

Pesach Lite, 2016

The Torah Empowerment Seminar, 2016

Siman Tov (Hebrew), 2016

The Fabric of Reality, 2016

Addendum, 2016

Fundamentals of Reincarnation, 2017

Reincarnation Clarified, 2016

All About Energy, 2017

What Goes Around, 2017

The God Experience, 2017

What in Heaven, 2017

The God Experience, Part 2, 2017

The God Experience, Part 3, 2017

It's About Time, 2017

Need to Know, 2017

Perceptions, Volume 2, 2017

Once Revealed, Twice Concealed, 2017

The Art of Chayn, 2017

A Matter of Laugh or Death, 2018

Geulah b'Rachamim Program, V. 1, 2018

Geulah b'Rachamim Program, V. 2, 2018

Geulah b'Rachamim Program, V. 3, 2018

Point of Acceptance, 2018
See Ya, 2018
In Discussion: Bereishis, 2018
Reincarnation Again, 2018
A Separate Matter, 2018
In Discussion: Shemos, 2019
A Search for Self, 2019
A Search for Trust, 2019
In Discussion: Bamidbar, 2019
How It Might Play Out, 2019
In Discussion: Vayikra, 2019
Where Are My Emotions Now, 2019
In Discussion: Devarim, 2019
The Early Years, 2019
Oh, So Blind, 2019
Not So Bad? 2019
Sha'ar HaPesukim: Shemos, 2019
The Fix, 2020
Sha'ar HaPesukim: Bereishis, 2020
Preparing For Redemption, 2020
Mindfulness, Torah & Redemption, 2020
Moment of Moments, 2020
My Zaidy's Diary, 2020
My Writing, Your Book, 2020

Any questions, especially regarding the dedication of an upcoming book, project, webinar, etc., should be sent to pinchasw@thirtysix.org.

Essays, books, video, audio & presentations that will change the way you look at history—and yourself.